Eureka!

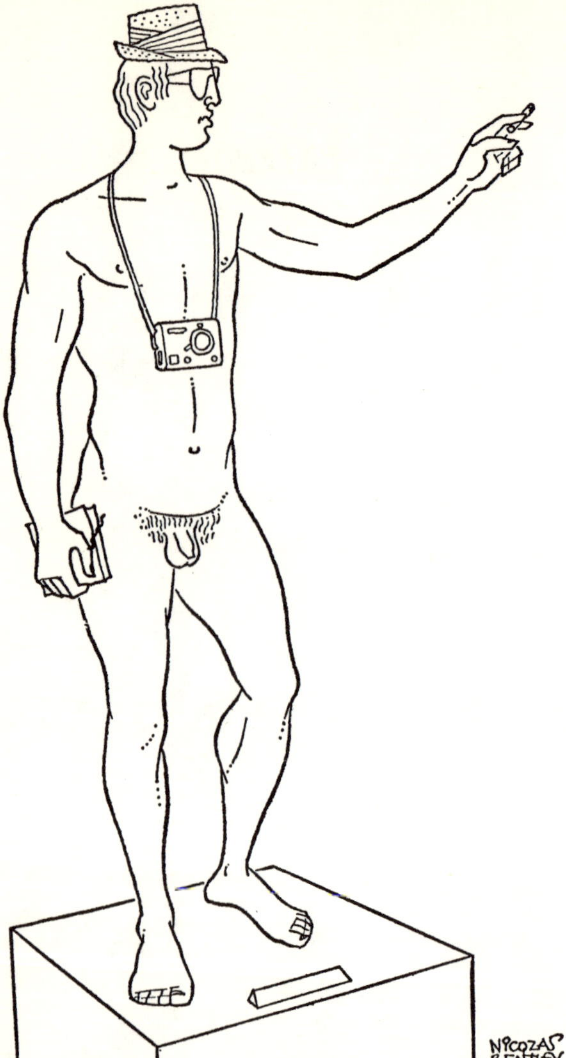

Homo touristicus

Eureka!

Rummaging in Greece

GEORGE MIKES

Nicolas Bentley
drew the pictures

ANDRE DEUTSCH

FIRST PUBLISHED JUNE 1965 BY
ANDRE DEUTSCH LIMITED
105 GREAT RUSSELL STREET
LONDON WC1
SECOND IMPRESSION APRIL 1974

PRINTED AND BOUND IN GREAT BRITAIN BY
REDWOOD BURN LIMITED
TROWBRIDGE AND ESHER

ISBN 0 233 95745 6

Contents

Homo Touristicus

If – like me – you visit Athens after a gap of fifteen years, you just won't recognize the place. Gone are the innumerable beggars, gone are the young mothers who used to gape through the restaurant windows, infant on arm, and look right into your mouth as you ate your steak. That is, if you *could* eat your steak under such supervision. Gone are . . . Well, it is not so much the details: it is the atmosphere that has completely changed. That miserable, hungry, depressed town which had just emerged from the war, to be plunged into an equally terrible civil war, has vanished and has been transformed into a prosperous, busy, bustling and affluent city, the traffic chaos and parking problems of which might be the envy of many a Western metropolis.

What is the reason for this amazing metamorphosis? There are, of course, several factors; no change has just one reason. The whole world is much better off than in 1949; the Greeks, it seems, must have worked hard, etc, etc. Yet, there can be no doubt, the main single factor is tourism. Even in the early fifties only archaeologists, classical scholars and a few eccentrics visited Greece. In 1953 the drachma was devalued, the country became really cheap for foreigners, and Greece made a bid for tourists. (In terms of money, this bid means that while in 1951 they were spending three million drachmas on tourist promotion, now they are spending more than a hundred million.) The bid was not quite as successful as it could have been, but it was successful enough. Round-faced travellers with crew-cuts or tweeds, smoking long cigars or pipes, carrying a photo-camera, a cine-camera and binoculars round their necks, started invading the peninsula and the islands in increasing numbers. Women in shorts and in bikinis appeared on the beaches; women in trousers appeared in the streets. In a country where one drachma – less than our late farthing – is still considerable value (this is, for example, the price a vine-grower is given for a pound of superb grapes), people noticed with amazement how strangers threw their money about, acting as though ten-pence or one shilling were no great sums. A page boy in the Hilton Hotel in Athens could make more money by opening the door to the right person with the right bow than a peasant family in Thrace could from a week's hard work. More and more people came – hotels and roads were built, more and more taxis, cars for hire, ships and ferry-boats, waiters, cleaners, foreign magazines and dancing girls were required, a souvenir-industry sprang into existence, and slowly, very slowly, even that peasant family in Thrace started feeling the benefit of those insultingly large tips, thrust into the hand of the little page boy in Athens.

The relationship between native and tourist is that of mutual contempt – a solid and reliable basis for a lasting friendship. The tourists (98 per cent of them, in my calculation) look down upon the natives and are inclined to judge the civilization of a country according to the smoothness or otherwise of its plumbing system, forgetting that the

Ladies of Athens rejoicing at the amenities afforded them by the Hilton Hotel

Palace of King Minos at Knossos had a faultless system of flushing lavatories at a time when not only New York or London but even the Athens of antiquity was yet to be built. When this is pointed out to the tourist, he replies with a little impatience but, one must admit, to the point, that five thousand years ago, no doubt, Knossos was the right place to visit; but he wants proper sanitation *now*. (Very well, they are being built at amazing speed, all over the country – four hundred good hotels in the last ten years.) The tourist may also find certain market-places in Northern Macedonia less hygienic than the average supermarket in Iowa; he is driven to the conclusion that *moussaka* is different from Southern fried chicken, *dolmades* is unlike steak-and-kidney pudding, *ouzo* is not whisky, and he wishes fervently that the Greeks kept their resin for the bows of their violins instead of putting it in their wine. Night-clubs, too, are decidedly inferior to those in Las Vegas. The tourist feels immensely superior to the Greeks and fails to realize – even dimly – that his main reason for coming here, as well as for going to many other places is – just to feel superior. To bask in the feeling of one's own superiority is infinitely more satisfying and more attractive than basking even in the warm Mediterranean sunshine.

But the natives' view of the tourists is much more devastating. The tourist may look down upon the Greeks for not speaking English, but, after all, it was the Greeks who used to call *all* those who did not speak Greek, barbarians. (Indeed, the word *barbarian* originates from the imitation of the barking *bar-bar* sound, which is how all foreign tongues sounded to a civilized Greek.) The tourists also *look* strange:

not only because their women wear trousers and strut about half naked, but also because in their newly-acquired Greek folk-costumes (and men in their wide-brimmed straw-hats) they look comical and undignified; much too ready, almost keen to give up their own identity and turn themselves into a parody of the native. They throw their money about recklessly and stupidly, and any child could take advantage of them to the tune of several drachmas. (But they don't; neither children nor grown-ups. The Greeks are extremely honest in such matters, and in ninety-nine cases out of a hundred they will run after you from a shop with the right change if you – or they – have made a mistake. It is a great pleasure to cheat someone, however slightly, with your cleverness; life is a battle and you must keep on winning all the battles, big and small, all the time. It is fun to sell some gullible tourists 'the very pebbles' Demosthenes held in his mouth when practising elocution on the Athenian shore; but to take advantage of a mistake is definitely *infra dig.*) It is not only the way the tourist spends his money: it is wrong and immoral – perhaps not even quite honest – to *have* so much. And then, of course, the tourist puts himself at a tremendous disadvantage simply by coming here. Hasn't he travelled thousands of miles *to be where the native is in any case*? Hasn't he travelled thousands of miles from his own dull, miserable country to gape at things that are so familiar to the native that he does not even throw a casual glance at them when passing by?

If the tourist smiles at the native, the native positively roars at the tourist. What is the little peasant boy – newly recruited and trained as a guide on some small island – to think when he shows a Christian church to a group, explains that it was built in the year 400 and some thoughtful member of the group asks him, 'Before or after Christ?' Or what is that other guide to think who explained to the American group he was taking round the Parthenon that it was not always a ruin, adding, 'In fact, not so long ago the Parthenon was covered'; a remark that prompted the enquiry: 'By a Greek company or an American one?' (On a much more serious level, I feel that this new species, the *Homo Touristicus* deserves more earnest attention than he receives.)

The native, in his turn, may also be a less serene and less dignified figure than he imagines himself. I am convinced that tourism itself – this post-war mania for travelling – is a major blessing for humanity. Perhaps the discovery of the wheel was the last event of equal importance. And the wheel, since its discovery, has never been put to better use than taking people – with cameras round their necks, straw-hats on their heads – to distant lands for no particular reason, for no particular purpose.

I am not talking now of the economic importance of tourism. This is obvious.

The social significance of tourism is a shade less conspicuous. The population of some of the Cyclades islands had been decreasing for a hundred years; then, after the beginning of the Tourist Era, it became stationary and now it is slowly increasing. Mykonos for one is definitely, booming. People, instead of leaving these islands, come back to enjoy the benefits of the tourist boom. This, of course, is not a purely economic matter: it makes a great difference – socially and psychologically – whether one's island is slowly and painfully dying or is looking forward to a prosperous future. Another social change: the castle, or the big house, has ceased to be the centre of village life; its place has been taken by the hotel. It is no longer the big landowner who can offer people jobs; it is the hotel. Apart from jobs, interesting things keep happening in the hotel; nothing ever happens in the Big House. Feudalism is being replaced not by Capitalism, as was the case almost all over Europe, but by Hotelism and Motelism. There was no Industrial Revolution in Greece; what we are now witnessing is a no less important Touristic Revolution.

People may – and indeed do – laugh at the tourist but they also emulate him. Greeks have also started to travel inside their own country. Thus their own image of Greece changes; and when the image changes, Greece changes, too. At the same time, goods improve, all sorts of services – bus and train connections, roads, medical services – become better: the Greeks must please their tourists; but the local people benefit just as much.

But it is first and foremost in *politics* that the tremendous importance of tourism is being felt. Tourism has, unobtrusively and almost unnoticed, become a major political factor, an influence for good. If General Franco's régime in Spain has become more liberal and tolerant, there are several reasons for the change, but the dominant influence is tourism. Franco must avoid abusive headlines branding him as a Fascist: it is bad for tourism. The obsession of all Communist countries with spies was growing into a sad joke. Not so long ago it was practically impossible for a private visitor to penetrate behind the Iron Curtain; today,

Communist countries are relaxing visa regulations: they are keen on receiving as many potential spies as might dare to come. In other words, they too are fighting for tourists. Many international quarrels, which would have proved eruptive a few years ago, were hurriedly patched up: they threatened the flow of tourists, so governments had no time for such quarrels. Let us take the Cyprus question as an example. The Greeks keep on declaring that they will never give up principles for the sake of expediency. This, I am sure, is true. Yet, there are ways and ways of insisting on principles and it is more than likely that relations between Greece and Britain would be much worse if the threat to tourism did not over-hang these problems.

Tourism has become a major cooling and moderating factor in world politics. People who used to hanker after a romantic and heroic death on the battlefield and drew their swords at the slightest provocation, think first of the tourist revenue today, and then sheath their swords in reflective, even mellow mood. Tourism makes people more cosmopolitan and less belligerent. Hostility between nations used to thrive on the sabre-rattlings of weak governments who either needed cheap successes or were determined to avert attention from grave internal problems; it flourished on a primitive, artificially fostered hatred and on poverty and ignorance. Foreign nations were painted as a collection of bogey-men and monsters. But nowadays more and more people visit this and that country; they meet waiters, shop-keepers, hotel-porters and, if they are lucky, a few civil servants, ironmongers and chartered accountants, on the beaches or in cafés. Nowadays all the visitors know that their host-nation consists of ordinary human beings – not altogether admirable, perhaps, not too bright – but on the whole kind and decent people, rather as we imagine ourselves to be. Thanks to tourism the world today lacks the madness and the stupid and blind hatred which were indispensable for engendering international crises of the Hitler variety. We just remember the head-waiter in our holiday hotel and refuse to sing martial songs; we remember the boy selling deck-chair tickets on the beach and feel disinclined to march; we remember the lady in the newspaper and titbit-shop and flatly refuse to accept her as a wicked international schemer and war-monger.

Tourism has the same effect in hotter climates – in the tourist countries themselves. There was in Athens a sweet-shop called Piccadilly. During the Cyprus troubles of 1963 and early 1964, people just would not tolerate a name like that, so the shop was re-named Cyprus. A few months later it reverted to its original name and became Piccadilly again. Nobody noticed this; or if they did, they could not have cared less. They were too busy. International friction is rather time-consuming. People just cannot spare the time to take part in demonstrations and listen to gutter-orators; or even to serious and sincere ones: deck-chairs have to be mended, garden furniture repainted, hotel lounges redecorated, etc, etc, for the next tourist season.

Is it then possible that where serious, gloomy and pompous diplomats have failed throughout the ages, silly tourists – with cameras and binoculars hanging round their necks and long cigars sticking out of their half-open mouths – will gloriously succeed without even trying? Is it in fact true that without giving one single thought to the problem, basking in the sunshine on various beaches and buying silly hats and idiotic souvenirs from slightly crooked shopkeepers, they are really preserving the peace of the world?

How to be a Greek

Lesson for Beginners

It is easy to spot the tourists; it is also easy to notice the *country*, which varies from lush to rugged but is always lovely. But a large number of people never notice the *Greeks*. Of course, they realize that there are people in the background who are busy doing things and helping to make their holidays enjoyable. They are vaguely aware of them, just as in the theatre one is vaguely aware of the stage-hands without whom – one knows – there would be no performance. Just as in the theatre some people have to push furniture about and raise and lower the curtain, so here, too, someone must prepare the meals, clean the rooms, and man the pleasure steamers. But they are not really *part* of the scene; they are not really essential. You may go on discussing a performance of *Hamlet* for hours without even mentioning the stage-hands; and you may go on relating details of a holiday in Corfu or Mykonos without mentioning or remembering the Greeks. For thousands and thousands it would make no difference if they were not there at all. In Britain they notice the British; in France they are fully aware of the French. But in Greece vast numbers do not realize that they are surrounded by fascinating, intelligent and likeable people, worthy of anybody's attention.

If by sheer luck, or extraordinary powers of observation,

you do discover that the Greeks exist and are, as a matter of fact, present in Greece in considerable numbers, and you start making enquiries as to what sort of people they are, you will be told that they are a people of contrasts; and further, that Greece is a land of contrasts. There is, indeed, one dominant impression I have culled during my travels: *all lands are lands of contrasts.* People will always inform you of this fact – that their country, Brazil or Sweden, Australia or Liechtenstein, is a land of contrasts; they will tell you this with an air of superior perception, as if they had just made a great discovery – indeed, coined a phrase. It used to be my ambition to find one single country which was not a land of contrasts. I gave up the futile search: no such country exists. What people mean is that there is love and hate, riches and poverty, gaiety and gloom, in their country. All of which are, of course, two sides of the same coin. One may as well declare that a shilling is a coin of contrasts because it has two faces.

'We are partly Eastern, partly Western; partly Oriental, partly Mediterranean,' a Greek friend assured me. 'Anyone who can't understand this, can't understand Greece.'

'Where is the Oriental in *you*?' I asked him.

'No Oriental in *me*,' he shouted angrily. 'I am purely Western. I am speaking of other Greeks.'

Very well, I said to myself, sighed, and resigned myself to this land-of-contrasts business. I gave in. If you want to be a Greek, you must be a man of contrasts. In case you really want to be a Greek, here are some further elementary rules for you.

Be courteous and dignified. Be unlike the Italians and

Contrasts

rather like the Catalans. Ooze old-fashioned politeness; be helpful; be chivalrous. But if anyone is in your way in the street or any public place, push him aside. Not aggressively, not arrogantly, but just as you might push a swing-door. And do not lose your temper when you notice that people are treating you as if *you* are a swing-door. People have nothing personal against swing-doors; some even like swing-doors. But you must push them if you want to get through. And, needless to say, no one would dream of saying 'sorry' to a swing-door.

A little more contrast: the ways of Greek shopkeepers are very un-Turkish and un-Arabic. They will not pull you into shops, they will not persuade you to buy. You may stand in front of their shop-windows for hours: the shopkeeper may contemplate you with equal interest, but he will not invite you in. Yet, you may go to do a bit of shopping – for a television set, for some furniture, or even for smaller items – and your prosperous Greek friend, accompanying you, will ask the shopkeeper – in your hearing and without a shade of embarrassment: 'And what about my commission?'

There are elements of contrast in the Greek muddle, too. At first you will regard it as typically Balkan; then, on reflection, as typically British. No doubt it contains strong Balkano-British elements.

Suppose you are looking on your tourist map for University Street, one of the main thoroughfares in Athens. You must first of all remember that all the street names are translated into English in such a way that they bear no resemblance to the actual names on the signs. Your eye lights on Akademias. But, you decide, Akademias cannot be University, so you continue the search and find University Street. But you are only half-way: the name will not be written out in English: University Street. You are proud of your classical education and your ability to read Greek, so you want to know what is actually on the street-signs. Comparing yours with a proper Greek map, you find that University Street is called Panepistimou. With the help of your two maps, you finally reach the street. This *must* be it, you decide, yet the street-signs inform you that you are in Venizelos Street. In some despair, you stop someone and explain your plight. He will tell you with a superior and patronizing smile that this, in fact, is University Street, alias Panepistimou. It used to be called Venizelos Street, but that was long, long ago. It's just that they've failed to change the street-signs in the last twenty years, that's all. Why hurry?

To be Greek you must acquire a great deal of charm and sense of Western humour. Yet, not forgetting the obligatory contrasts, even if you are ready to laugh at others – often quite loudly and maliciously – you must remain Oriental enough never to laugh at yourself. Others are fair targets; but not you. And you are, of course, right; after all, there is nothing – nothing at all – funny or ridiculous about you.

Admire yourself unreservedly. Most Greeks regard themselves as Apollos, which is, after all, modest enough; they could regard themselves as Zeuses. I met few young men who were not convinced that they would become Cabinet ministers, great scholars, or millionaires – preferably all three. And I never met one single Greek – young or old – who was not convinced that he would make a better Prime Minister than any Greek Prime Minister in any age, past or future, with the possible exceptions of Venizelos and Pericles. We, all of us, tend to cherish pretty flattering opinions of ourselves (or manage to cover up our feelings of inferiority more or less successfully, which comes to the same thing). But if we are proud of our physical beauty, we may suspect that our intellect lags behind the greatest, that we fall short of the Einstein class; or if we regard ourselves as leading intellectual lights, we may admit that our physical beauty might not qualify us to become Miss (or Mister) Universe. We know, deep down, that there are at least *some* subjects about which other people might know more. Most of us, for example, are ready to admit that we are not quite up to date in molecular biology and we feel – rightly or wrongly – that such an admission does not entail any great loss of face. Not so the Greeks. They are equally well versed in all subjects under the sun. They will mention, with broad grins, the days of the Russo-Japanese war – which was followed in Greece with passionate interest – when there was not a single Greek newspaper, Athenian or provincial, which failed to give detailed advice on matters of high strategy to the Russian Commander-in-Chief. And, of course, they would never be so biased as not to guide, with equal fervour, the admirals of the Imperial Japanese Navy.

Few people will doubt your true Greek omniscience and none will object to it. That is one of the secrets of the Greek. To be conceited and disagreeable is easy; to be conceited and keep your charm – and even modesty – is a much more complicated affair.

If you want to be a Greek, throw your sense of timing to the winds. Time does not mean much in the Mediterranean lands, and how right and civilized their attitude to Time is. Our own smug punctuality means that we are slaves of Time. A free man's life should not be governed by the clock. Life is a struggle against Time, in any case – why give in without a proper fight? A Greek friend will tell you: 'We'll come at eight tonight,' then add with a grin, 'Greek time, not English time': meaning the Time of Free Man, which is completely independent of the clock. It is understood that 'eight o'clock on Tuesday' may mean any hour, on any day of the week, except eight o'clock on Tuesday. The trouble starts when people drop in on you for ten minutes and stay for four or five hours without blinking an eyelid. There is something affectionate and solicitous in their care for you: they have come because you are a foreigner, a guest in their country and you may feel lonely. The possibility that you – an unfriendly northerner – *long* to be lonely never enters their mind. 'We'll come on Sunday afternoon again,' they will say, and leave you in a state of utter exhaustion. You love them; you appreciate their kindness; you are fond of their company. But Sunday? Isn't that just a wee bit too soon to meet again? You need not worry about Sunday. They will not come on Sunday. They will drop in on Friday *and* Saturday for the customary five or six hours. They thought that being a stranger you might need some help and advice – you might be lonely. They will also bring you a charming present. You truly love them. That you feel a strong desire to strangle them at the same time, only shows what a nasty and ungrateful creature you are bascially.

If you seriously think of becoming a Greek, you must get rid of your English shyness, reserve, and inclination to be taciturn. It just will not do. These are legitimate, indeed, the most common opening gambits for conversations between perfect strangers:

'What's your name?'

'How much do you earn?'

'How much rent do you pay?'

'Are you married?'

'How many children do you have?'

'Are you on good terms with your in-laws? Did they pay your dowry in full?'

(If you are a man and say you are not married, they wink at you with an understanding grin, implying that you must have a beautiful mistress; they may even ask, in fact often do: 'Is she fair or dark?' If you are a woman they say, 'Why not?')

Immediately after the war these questions led to grave misunderstandings – sometimes even to blows – between the British forces and the Greek population. The British, very security-minded as always, had been specially warned not to give information to strangers. When the Greeks asked them where they came from, what engagements they had taken part in and where they were going next, the British decided that the whole country was chock-full of spies.

Least said, soonest mended

But in spite of their curiosity, the Greeks are no good at all as spies; and hopeless as material to be spied upon. One of the German chiefs of intelligence – I do not remember his name – explained in his memoirs that there were two countries in which German intelligence had totally and hopelessly failed during the war: Japan and Greece. The Japanese talked too little; the Greeks talked too much.

A Painful Discovery

I was listening to a telephone conversation in the office of a high-ranking government official. He sounded kind and understanding, yet practically every other word he said was: '*Ne, ne*.'

'Poor man,' I thought, meaning the supplicant at the other end of the wire.

When my friend finished, I told him: 'You sounded a bit negative.'

He smiled. He knew what I had in mind and explained: 'Oh no. *Ne, ne*, means *yes, yes*, in Greek.'

'Surely not,' I told him. 'I should hate to argue with you about the meaning of a Greek word – and a fairly well-known word at that. But that is just impossible. In every language in the world the negative begins with an *n*; the affirmative *never*. In fact, the very word *ne* – or something very near it – does mean *no* in a number of languages. You don't mean to tell me . . .'

He interrupted me with a tolerant and slightly self-conscious smile on his face. He looked like a man who had been caught out: 'I do mean to tell you *ne* means *yes* in Greek.'

'Well, you seem to be pretty adamant about it,' I wavered. Then seeing a faint glimmer of hope, I added: 'It did not mean that in ancient Greek?'

'Yes, indeed it did. It is part of our heritage.'

What could I say to that? I admire the Greeks; I love the Greeks. I love them dearly. But let's face it: you just cannot trust a nation which says *ne*, *ne* and means yes, yes.

How to be a Greek

Lesson for the Advanced Class

If you seriously aspire to become a Greek, you must be politically minded. Like all new nations, the Greeks are great nationalists. I know they are pretty ancient for a new nation (yes, I have heard of Homer); on the other hand, modern Greece as an independent nation was born only in the nineteenth century.

Their chauvinism may sometimes take you a little aback. Now that they are quarrelling with the Turks over Cyprus, Turkish coffee has been renamed Greek coffee; Turkish Delight has become Greek Delight. When you protest that Turkish coffee must be Turkish coffee, however Dr Kutchuk may behave, they retort: 'Nonsense! It never was Turkish in the first place. They took it over from us in Byzantine times.'

In addition to being ardent nationalists, they are passionately interested in day-to-day politics and you must not be surprised if a little shoe-shine boy opens a conversation with you by remarking: 'If I were Prime Minister . . .'

Their love of politics is closely connected with their love of arguments. If you want to be a Greek worthy of the name, you must be ready to argue with ardour about anything and everything. The Greeks blow up quickly, they shout and howl and roar at one another, their eyes flash, they grind their teeth. This state of ferocious excitement may be provoked by someone upsetting a glass of water or not closing the door properly. Then, it is all over in a flash: they calm down as quickly as they flare up and peace reigns again. The issue very often is simply this: who is to be blamed? (I think it is a silly point in most cases, typical of the Orient as well as of British political parties.) If you do not understand the language, some quarrels may sound farcical to you. I was buying something in a stationery shop when in came a gentleman who made a small purchase. Before you could say Aristotle, the shopkeeper and his customer were almost at each other's throats. They bawled angrily at each other and I was prepared for blows or bloodshed at any moment. But suddenly the row stopped, the man picked up his parcel, shook hands with the shopkeeper in the friendliest manner and left. There had been no angry argument; there had been no argument at all. What I had heard was an amicable if lively exchange of ideas.

On another occasion I was standing with some friends at the counter in a taverna, when two strangers started talking to each other, rather tentatively. In no time they were quarrelling fiercely, both of them getting ready for murder.

'What were they quarrelling about?' I asked one of my friends later.

'About the weather,' he replied.

The answer surprised me a little. How could two strangers strike up such a violent quarrel about the most innocuous of subjects? So I pressed my friend and he explained:

'Oh, it was nothing, really. One of them started off with the usual enquiries about the other's income and sex-life – so all was well. Then he remarked that the weather was getting colder. The other agreed and added that winter was approaching much too early this year. Alas, he went on, heating was getting dearer and dearer which was a disgrace and entirely the fault of the government. Upon which the first man blew up and said, not at all, it was all the fault of the previous government. And so on. Just a little dispute: there were no casualties.'

If you want to take part in a Greek quarrel you must learn how to use the Greek type of argument. One day I was buying some Turkish – I am sorry – some Greek Delight. The cheaper sort of this commodity aimed at the vulgar taste is unadorned; the better sort is full of almonds. I have a vulgar taste and insisted on the simple sort; the girl insisted on selling me the almond-studded type. 'I want the one without almonds,' I told her.

'This is without almonds,' she said firmly, pointing to the almond type.

Normally I prefer to believe other people's words rather than the evidence of my own eyes, but in this case I was not quite convinced.

'Is it?' I asked incredulously.

' 'Course,' she said a little uppishly. 'You take the almonds out like this (and she demonstrated) and then it is without almonds. D'you see?'

I did see and bought the stuff, as told to. I am sure selling that to me must have been sheer Greek Delight.

To complete your education, you have to be:

(1) *Generous.* The Greeks are a truly hospitable and generous people. They have a saying about themselves: a Greek will either steal your shirt or give you his own. My shirt was never once stolen, but there were innumerable occasions when somebody else's shirt was forced upon me.

(2) *Suspicious.* Suspicion is a basic trait of the Greek character. A friend explained: 'A Greek has to be suspicious if he wants to survive.' Another friend, a psycho-analyst collecting data about the Greek character, asked some people: 'What would you do if a stranger spoke to you in a dream?'

One man thought this over and declared firmly: 'It would be no use his trying, I never speak to strangers.'

Another said: 'I should ask for his identification papers.'

The third smiled modestly: 'Talk to *me*? . . . Am I *that* important?'

(3) You have to be *superstitious.* However enlightened and westernized, there are certain superstitions which . . . one does not take them seriously, of course, but . . . how shall we put it? – well, it's just better to be on the safe side. *Throwing the five* is the most awful of all curses. *Throwing the five* is casting an evil spell by turning your open palm, with the five fingers stretched apart, to someone. If it is thrown at you, you must throw it back immediately and then all is well; but if you fail to do so, only some complicated cleansing ceremony can save you. On one occasion, I heard, all the market traders, fishwives, male and female customers, the lot, fled in panic from a provincial market because a middle-aged English lady threw the five on the entire populace. She did not mean to, of course; all she

meant to do was to signal to her friend, some distance away, that the price of grapes was five drachmas. No one questioned her integrity; but integrity does not matter. The market place had to be closed down and ceremonially cleansed. On another occasion, a lorry driver was charged with dangerous driving because he had run into a lamp-post. His defence was that he had got into some altercation with a van driver who had thrown the five at him. Naturally, he had to throw it back straight away to save himself from trouble. While saving himself from trouble, he hit the lamp-post. His defence was accepted and he was acquitted.

(4) Finally, if you want to be a Greek you have to be *clever*. Very, very clever. The Greeks are sharp; very quick on the uptake; and fully aware of their cleverness. Their quickness of mind is really fabulous. A Greek diplomat, who had taken some part in the preliminary negotiations for Greece's joining the Common Market as an associate member, told me:

'We had to negotiate mostly with Dutchmen. For me, the talks had two unforgettable characteristics. The first was the difference between the ways our minds worked. It was almost pathetic. God, those Dutchmen are stodgy and slow. We knew what they were going to say long before they'd finished a sentence. But they went on, labouring every point with endless patience, stodgily, dully, harping on the obvious. Yes, I'm afraid, stodgy is the word for them.'

'And the other?'

'What other?' he asked me, surprised. 'What do you mean?'

'You said the talks had two unforgettable characteristics. One was the slowness and stodginess of the Dutchmen. What was the other?'

'Oh, yes, the other . . .' he said airily. 'Well, the other was that these slow and stodgy Dutchmen gained all their points. Every single one of them. And we lost all ours.'

Foreigners Only

A lot of water has flowed through the Corinth Canal since the days of the Peloponnesian War, when the Greeks regarded all foreigners as barbarians, suitable only to be slaves and not worthy of much consideration. But the *spirit* of those days, when all Greeks regarded themselves as individuals – not just members of a herd with no voice and no rights of their own – is very much alive.

In Zalakosta Street, where the government's Press Department is situated and where foreign journalists come and go at all times, parking is allowed on one side of the street. But the parking sign carries an unusual qualification. It says: FOR FOREIGNERS ONLY.

The sign does not actually say: FOR BARBARIANS ONLY. It uses the friendlier word: *xenos*.

Can you imagine a similar sign in London? When such a sign goes up somewhere in Britain – extending privileges to aliens while denying them to Britons – then even the most obstinate British day-dreamers will realize that the days of Britannia's ruling the waves and the world are over. A 'FOR FOREIGNERS ONLY' sign would bring home this fact more forcefully than the appearance of an African gunboat off our shores and an African admiral – as the leader of a landing party – ordering the whipping of our Prime Minister for having failed to treat some visiting African tribal chief with due consideration.

Not that the Greeks approve of that sign in Athens. One day, a friend of mine came to see me in my hotel in a state of considerable excitement. He is a Greek, and drives a car with a Greek number-plate, which he had parked in Zalakosta Street, in the heart of Athens, about two hours earlier. After dealing with some business, he returned to his car to fetch some books he wanted to show me. A policeman was waiting for him.

'I'll have to report you. This parking space is for foreigners only,' the policeman told him.

Such a statement always sparks off a lengthy and heated discussion in Greece. The offender – whatever the offence – cries to the heavens; points out the injustice of the traffic regulations and/or the entire legal system; explains that it is really the fault of the other fellow (if there is another fellow involved); appeals to the policeman's sympathy; reminds him that he, the policeman, too has a family, etc, etc. My friend was no exception. In the course of his passionate peroration, he asked the policeman:

'For "Foreigners Only"! And you are telling me that this is fair and just?'

He received a surprising reply:

'Oh no. I'm telling you that it is very wrong.'

My friend, sensing victory or, at least, a chance of escaping, pricked up his ears. It was the policeman's turn now to plunge into rhetoric.

'Whoever heard of such a sign in a capital city with any self-respect? Forbidding our own citizens to do something which is permitted to foreigners. Turning our own people into second-class citizens. It's unheard-of, it's shameful.'

'Well, then . . .' my friend suggested hopefully.

'There is no "well then" . . . I didn't make this regulation. I hate it. But my job is to enforce it, whatever my personal feelings. Your driving licence, please.'

My friend started to lose his patience:

'Well, what are you complaining about it for? Enforce it, if you must. But can't you keep your personal views to yourself!'

The policeman drew himself up to his full height and spoke with dignity:

'*You* started arguing with me. Why do *you* think I'm interested in *your* views? I assure you, putting on this uniform does not deprive me of my rights as a free citizen of a free country. I can express my views whether you like them or not; and whatever I, myself, think of the laws I've got to enforce –'

He stopped for a second, then continued more informally once again:

'My purely personal guess is that the infringement of these disgusting and revolting regulations will cost you about two hundred drachmas.'

When my friend arrived at my hotel, still heated and rather upset after his encounter with the policeman, and told me his story, I felt like exclaiming, 'Long live Pericles!'

Plato's Revenge

It is silly to pretend that a classical education has no practical advantages. But for my classical upbringing, I should have been lost and quite unable even to guess which lavatory to enter: the one marked GYNAIKON or the one marked ANDRON. Thanks to Homer and Ignatius Steller (the latter being my erstwhile Greek master), when the call came, I hesitated not.

A classical education gives an immense feeling of superiority. You feel like a fountain of knowledge when you are able to tell your wife that the mysterious sign ΘOHNAI simply means Athens and ΦESTIBAL stands for nothing more impressive than Festival. You can read the newspapers, too. You do not understand a single word of what they say, but you can *read* them. This makes you the proper counterpart of the illiterate Greek peasant, who can understand every word but cannot read them.

Your reading will not be too fluent in the first few days. It is with great joy that you recognize – after a lengthy effort – that one name hidden behind those forbidding classical letters is that of a well-known but common brand of petrol, while another one is the name of that detergent which washes whitest of all. The detergent may be something of a bore at home; but it does take on a bit of an aura when it looks, at first sight, like a quotation from Plato. On the other hand, having deciphered the name: Bank of

Attica, I felt deeply disappointed. The history of Attica, yes; the glory of Attica, yes. But the *Bank* of Attica?

Best fun of all – a game at which I have spent many delightful hours – is deciphering the names of English and American film-stars. Transliteration into Greek is not a simple task. The Greeks partly lack and have partly lost a number of letters. The ancient *beta*, for example, is read as a *v* today and as a result, there is no letter representing *b* in modern Greek. So they have had to invent one and they decided – for some unfathomable reason – that *mp* should be read as *b*. So when you see the curious word: MPAR, do not be deterred: it is simply pronounced BAR, which is what it means. They have no *d* (the *delta* is really a *th*-sound today) nor *g* (either hard or soft), nor the *sh*-sound. So, with a number of unlisted difficulties added, every English (and other foreign) word or name becomes a puzzle. To decipher the name of Greta Garbo or Harold Lloyd (they show a lot of delightful old films in Athens) is a major feat. My greatest achievement was to get the name of the late Hungarian comedian Szoke Szakall. It looks formidable enough in English: in Greek it is positively terrifying.

Try as hard as you can, it is impossible to forget that you are in the land of ancient myth and culture. Night-clubs and low joints are named after Dionysos and Apollo; soaps and lavatory cleansers bear the names of Zeus and Hermes; insurance companies seem to have a great deal in common with Aphrodite, and makers of soft drinks and boiled sweets dote on Agamemnon and Hephaistos. In the great American hotel, you can order a Venus-parfait (in the Byzantine Café) and at a seaside taverna I could enjoy a red mullet *à la* Prometheus. I shudder to think what is going to happen to the venerable inhabitants of Mount Olympus when commercial television arrives in Greece. (At the moment, there is no television of any kind; yet the dread day cannot be long delayed.) And if occasionally you still feel some doubt whether you really are in the land of Homer and Apollo, you will be reassured by meeting waiters called Themistocles, sponge-vendors called Socrates and by hearing little boys called Agamemnon being told off by their mothers in no classical terms (though your doubts re-emerge when you find out that Themistocles is known as Mitsos, that Socrates is, in fact, called Kosta and Agamemnon was christened George – or rather Georgios. Anyway, a noble effort should always be appreciated).

Sooner or later you are bound to ask yourself: how Greek are the Greeks? How closely are they related to their great ancestors? If you ask other people, the answers will vary enormously. Ardent Greek patriots will aver that they are the direct descendants of the ancients; doubters and cynics will laugh this off: the Greeks, they declare with malicious glee, are a nation of goat-herds, a hotch-potch of nationalities and wild Balkan tribes, having nothing whatsoever to do with Socrates, Pythagoras or Sophocles. It is a silly old fallacy that the truth always lies half-way between two extremes, but in this case it seems to be at least true that the modern Greeks have more to do with the ancient Greeks than any other nation in the world. Whatever the truth of the matter, another question remains: *what if they are the direct descendants*? Does this fact ennoble them? Do we have to revere them on account of Aristotle,

Enjoyment of the reflected glory of Xenophon and Thucydides

who lived in the fourth century BC? I asked a Greek historian whether Greece has an aristocracy. Oh, no, he assured me with a superior smile, an aristocracy was a ridiculous anachronism. Why should we revere a person, he asked, because one of his remote ancestors did something meritorious a few centuries ago? But half an hour later he extolled the greatness of ancient Greece and, quite obviously, tried to bask in the reflected glory of Xenophon and Thucydides. We should, it seems, reject the notion of aristocratic families (who shone perhaps two and a half centuries ago) but should accept the idea of aristocratic nations (who had their great moments two and a half millennia ago).

If you scratch the surface and get under the skin of this problem, you will find that it is not as simple as it looks. The trouble is not that the Greeks have nothing to do with their great ancestors; but that they have much too much to do with them.

You cannot forget ancient Greece; *they* could, for a long time. Attica and the Peloponnese are, after all, the venues of their glories and achievements. Attica, where Athens stood (and stands), is much smaller than Kent, and Athens at the height of her glory and influence had a population considerably less than Birmingham has today. You cannot even attempt to summarize the achievements of the ancient Greeks in a few lines. The English like to believe that Shakespeare is the only dramatist of consequence; but Aeschylus, Sophocles, Euripides and Aristophanes preceded him by quite a few centuries. Phidias and Praxiteles were great artists; Pindar was no mean poet, and Homer was one of the greatest novelists – yes, I said novelist – ever born. Our philosophers are still engaged in arguments with Plato and Aristotle; our doctors are still taking the Hippocratic oath; our athletes still compete in the Olympic Games, and well, the list is endless. Their wisdom, their love of reason, their statecraft, their hatred of astrology, their political, literary, artistic and scientific achievements are almost overpowering. Yet, for a long time, all these memories meant very little for the modern Greeks. Byzantine memories meant much more: they were more real and more tangible. And, in the most important aspect, modern Greece has managed to do much better than the old one: the ancients never succeeded in forming a proper nation, and their factions and rivalries were their undoing. Modern Greece is not only a nation but in one respect is one of the most successful: since 1832, when the modern Greek state was founded, she has more than doubled her territory, emerging as victor in several wars and never losing a square inch. (The post-World War I loss to the Turks was only a deduction from their gains.)

After the rebirth of Greece, the ancient traditions had to be laboriously and artificially revived. Modern scholars wanted people to take pride in their past even if it was far from certain that it really was *their* past. The ancient alphabet was there as a solid foundation, but hardly anything else. The language of King Otto's Greece did not much resemble the language of Sophocles – even if, once again, it resembled it more than any other living tongue. But a Greek child did not find it any easier to learn Homer's language than a Bulgarian or a Norwegian child did – although he had to suffer much more while trying to do so because the subject was taken more seriously in Greece than anywhere else in the world. They pretended for a long time that Homer's language was their language with some slight changes; but this was nonsense. Why, if you say *hoi polloi* to a modern Greek child, he will not know what you are talking about. It was the present government that faced realities bravely and sensibly, threw pretence to the wind and ordered that the ancient masterpieces should be translated into, and taught in, modern Greek. This reform sparked off a noisy academic battle, with Athens University in the forefront, against the Government. It was generally accepted, however, that it is the ideas and the spirit of the Hellenic heritage that count, not the actual words and syntax of a dead language; that it is, in any case, more helpful to understand what you are reading than just to pretend to understand it (as do the majority of the pupils and, judging by my own experience, even a small minority of the teachers). It may well have been the case that killing ancient Greek – or almost killing it – was the most effective way of keeping it alive.

But the *spirit* and the *ideas* caused some difficulties, too. The revival of the classical spirit (which started, as I have mentioned, after 1832) was a success: perhaps the most unfortunate success in Greek history. It created a deadening tradition. To be a great man's son is a heavy burden; to be a descendant of those glorious and ingenious ancient Greeks proved to be almost fatal. Once you are convinced that Uncle Aristotle, Uncle Pythagoras, Uncle Solon and Uncle Pericles are members of your family – quite close relations, in fact – you tend to be satisfied with your own achievements and rest on their laurels. What modern nations are striving

Mrs Winslow T. Brewster, of Waxahachie, Texas, contemplating the ideas and the spirit of the Hellenic heritage

for today, in our nuclear and electronic age, you solved already some millennia ago. (Fortunately, the Greeks were not satisfied with the glory of Thermopylae, and in World War II they fought that famous battle over and over again, gaining the admiration and gratitude of the civilized world.)

A modern Greek does not need to be wise: Uncle Plato was wise enough for the whole family; Uncle Archimedes did his bit for physics, and Uncle Aeschylus and Uncle Herodotus wrote as well – if not better – than some of our modern playwrights or historians. If you are a modern Greek, you grow convinced that Uncle Socrates, Uncle Aristotle, Uncle Homer, Uncle Euripides, Uncle Pericles and all the other illustrious uncles *are really you, yourself.* You may be forgiven if your shoulders prove weak and even collapse under the burden of this glorious heritage. You may come to feel that your family has already done its bit for humanity; now it is up to other people to exert themselves, while you lie back and watch them with a critical eye.

Priests with Beards

I think I ought to declare that I used to be biased against all churches in general and against the Greek Orthodox Church in particular. The Church is a medieval institution which failed to move with the times half as successfully as certain other medieval institutions – Parliament or the Common Law, for example. I could never understand – to descend to a very minor point – why priests have to walk about in Victorian nightshirts of varying colours, instead of being dressed like the rest of us – silly, old-fashioned and impractical though our own garments may be. How an Archbishop can don a glorified and bejewelled chef's hat and keep a straight face, has always been beyond me. The Greek *papas* are dressed, not in Victorian but in Ottonian (King Otto, 1821–64) nightshirts, which are even worse.

I have, of course, nothing against the dogma of the Orthodox Eastern Church – nothing more, that is, than I have against other dogmas. I wonder if the Creed, which concerns theology proper – the doctrine of the essential nature of the God-head and the doctrine of the God-head in relation to manhood in the Incarnation – could arouse any wild excitement, even in patriarchal or exarchical circles today. But the Eastern Church was, after all, a political creation, like the Church of England. After the Roman Empire was split in two, the Church was bound to follow suit. This I fully understand; my aversion was based partly on ignorance, which has now been cleared up, and partly on personal prejudice, which unfortunately cannot be helped.

Let's take the case of my ignorance first. I always thought that the Orthodox Church was even more conservative, non-progressive and autocratic than the Roman. But it is not. The Roman Church is a despotic monarchy with one head, in whom all power rests; the Eastern Church is an oligarchy with seven patriarchs. I thought that the Orthodox Church was just as strict and old-fashioned in family matters as the Western Churches. I was wrong again. In matters concerning divorce and birth-control, the Roman Church still lives in the darkest Middle Ages, while the more go-ahead Western Churches have reached, at last, the later Middle Ages. The Greek Church is, however, more flexible than its counterparts and, naturally enough, much more Greek. It permits not only divorce but remarriage. Marriage in the West is still regarded as sacred – however difficult it is for the ordinary layman to see what is so sacred about it. In Greece *the first three* marriages are sacred, which is fairer to the congregation and more realistic, too. The Greek Church *blesses* the first marriage; *accepts* the second; *tolerates* the third; and *forbids* the fourth.

'This, in one single respect, is harsher on some people than the Roman rule,' a Greek friend explained. 'A fourth marriage is forbidden, in whatever manner the first three ended.'

'What do you mean?' I asked.

'It's quite clear. If a man loses three young wives in quick succession because all three die, he is not allowed to marry a fourth time. You must agree that this is terribly unjust.'

'No, I don't agree at all,' I replied. 'If a man loses three young wives in quick succession he is more likely than not to have had a hand in their deaths. The only person I can think of to whom such a tragedy befell is George Smith, the murderer of those unfortunate ladies who became known as the Brides in the Bath.'

'You are not being quite just,' my friend told me in a reflective voice.

If a man commits adultery or some other grave matrimonial offence, the ecclesiastical courts may forbid him to remarry for a specified period. This punishment, however, may be waived in exceptional circumstances.

'I was guilty of adultery,' another Greek friend told me. 'But in my case the punishment was waived.'

'What was so exceptional in your case?'

'Well, I wanted to remarry. I wished to marry the lady with whom I had committed adultery.'

This did not sound all that convincing to me. I told my friend that even in my limited experience this fact was not quite so exceptional as he tried to make out.

'Perhaps not,' he agreed, 'but the bishop is my father's best friend. And you must admit that is exceptional.'

Priests of the Orthodox Church cannot marry; but married men may become priests and in fact do. Promotion is barred to a married priest, but village priests – and *they* are the married ones – do not aspire to become monks or bishops. In fact, until recently, they had little or no ecclesiastical training and a fair number of them were illiterate. (Nowadays, two years' training in a seminary is compulsory.) The village priests must be married, because a celibate –

or at least unmarried – priest would become the laughing-stock of the place. These priests are peasants and must live the lives of fellow-peasants. They are very poor; they do not have much property. They must possess at least *something*, so they insist on owning a wife and a few children. They seem to be reasonably industrious; the most common name in Greece is Papadopoulos, which means, Son of the Priest.

The village priest's minimum stipend is under £20 per month, consequently his prestige is small. Such is life in Greece, such is life in Britain, in the United States, in the Congo, or any place one chooses to name. If the priest's income were raised to £200 or £2,000, his prestige would rise immediately and proportionately. If God had more ready money, this world of ours, in spite of its secular leanings, would revere His servants much more.

I found that I had also been wrong about the influence of the Greek Church. A provincial bishop is a pretty influential personage – he is chairman of every social institution in his see. If he insists on the building of, say, an Old People's Home, it will be built. But the bishop's political influence is limited. The Church could not order people how to vote – in fact, any such attempt, on a mass scale, would probably misfire with the obstinate and strongly individualistic Greeks. The Church, however, can still create a resounding row about immoral films or books; indeed, about all matters of secondary importance, but not about politics and economics. In fact, there are no religious political parties in Greece, as there are in so many other countries, from Germany to Israel.

It is true that a person before his christening is an un-person; a baby is an un-baby. One cannot obtain papers, identity cards, a driving licence, or any other kind of licence before one is registered with the Church; in other words, before one is baptized. One has no legal identity. No marriage concluded outside the Church is regarded as valid. Greek labourers go to West Germany in large numbers and marry German girls. Then they return to Greece – with or without their wives – where they are regarded as bachelors. In Greece, they can let the girl down with impunity and can even remarry in church. Should they return to Germany, however, they would be arrested for bigamy.

There are few Muslims in Greece (there are some Turks in Rhodes and in Western Thrace) and the number of Jews was tragically reduced by the Germans during the war. Greece is almost one hundred per cent Orthodox. There is no persecution of other religions; but there is slight discrimination: only a member of the Orthodox Church can rise to real prominence.

A formidable proportion of the population are church-goers. But church-going in the majority of villages is more of a social event than a religious one. Indeed, in many places, the Sunday service is the only social function of any importance. Sunday service has a tremendous advantage in a poor country: it is an entertainment free of charge. And it brings us back to the Greek paradox: the country is a land of practising Orthodox church-goers without too much ardent religious feeling; just as it is a monarchy without much feeling for the monarch.

Having discovered all this, I was driven to the conclusion that the Orthodox Church is less reactionary, indeed, is more liberal, tolerant, happy-go-lucky and politically less interfering than the churches of many other lands. Why then, was I so prejudiced against it? Why did I presume that the country was more priest-ridden than it really is? Why did I feel so apprehensive whenever I caught sight of a *papa*? And at last I understood: *it was their beards.*

I think I may state with a clear conscience that I feel no prejudice against any man because of his race, religion, nationality, profession, or social class – even if he is the eldest son of a marquess. But I am an anti-beard man. Perhaps an anti-hair-on-the-face man. Even a moustache makes me vaguely doubtful; beards make me wince. I do not hate bearded men; I do not wish to persecute them, deprive them of the vote, or exclude them from high office. I do not wish to deprive them of anything – not even of their beards. But I mistrust them. For me, a beard shows lack of sincerity. I always feel that a beard is there to cover up, to conceal something. For me, all beards are false beards.

Yet, beards used to have one tremendous, almost unique, advantage in my eyes. I have an extremely poor memory for faces. I never forget a *person*; I never forget a name; I always remember where I met someone and what we were talking about. But I can neither remember nor recognize his face. As some people are colour-blind, I am face-blind. But, of course, a beard is such a distinctive mark, that I never had any difficulty in recognizing bearded people. One just could not take Bernard Shaw for H. G. Wells; even I could not mix up Compton Mackenzie with Graham

Greene, Melvin Lasky with Stephen Spender, or Santa Claus or President Makarios with the Archangel Gabriel. On this count, I felt deeply obliged to bearded gentlemen.

In Greece I saw innumerable bearded priests everywhere and they made me restive. I met quite a few of them, I had to interview some *and I could not tell one from the other.* It was their very beards that confused and confounded me. All bearded priests looked exactly the same to me: young and old, short and tall, fat and slim – with the single exception of that dear and thoughtful divine who was kind enough to grow a red beard for my sake. The beard, my anchor, my former guiding light, my only reliable friend of old, was playing a cruel practical joke on me and proving my worst enemy.

A Belated Apostate

The Church – as I have said before – still belongs to the Middle Ages. The Church could find either of two remedies for this ill. It could modernize itself and bring itself up-to-date. But the better, healthier, and more attractive solution would be to leave the Middle Ages and return to antiquity; in other words, to revive the religion of the ancient Greeks. Surely, it was the most poetic, most progressive and most imaginative religion ever invented by man. We call it paganism today, but that is just mud-slinging – a nasty characteristic of a nasty age. The faith of the ancient Greeks contained a great deal of the essentials of modern religions; and all modern religions, in turn, are full of pagan relics. Books, indeed libraries, have been written about the psychology of paganism, superstition and modern religion – but this is of course not my subject. Without going deeply into this vast problem, it is worthwhile, however, throwing a glance at old Dionysos being transformed into St Dionysius, keeping his time-honoured connection, not only with wine, but even with the island of Naxos.

The faith of the ancient Greeks was not monotheistic, which has surprised many observers. They point out that the main characteristic of ancient Greek mentality was striving after logic, unity and system. How is it possible – they go on to ask – that in the course of their search for unity and system, the Greeks never arrived at monotheism?

The answer is simple: it is *because* they were logical and systematic. And also democratically minded. They rejected the idea of one omnipotent ruler on earth, and they did not accept one ruler on Olympus either. They believed in a Committee of Gods – each with his or her own department, sphere of authority, rights and duties. It was a small committee at first but – as committees are wont to do – it grew larger and more and more unwieldy. What could be more logical and systematic than a committee, with responsibilities properly allocated to all members? I shall never forget an American professor who once shouted, in an outburst of anger: 'This world is so unspeakably awful that it just cannot be ruled by one single God. It must be run by a committee!' The ancient Greeks must have thought the same.

How delightfully the ancient Greeks managed to solve certain problems for their gods – problems which we find beyond us. How much more intelligently they handled immigrant gods than we handle mortal immigrants. They just gave the foreign god an entry permit to Olympus and a working permit was attached to it. They accepted foreign gods and there was no discrimination against them whatever their colour or indeed creed. They knew, of course, that all gods are not equal, just as all men are not equal; but every foreign god had a fair chance. The Greeks worshipped them along with their own, made sacrifices to them and kept them happy. Those Greek gods and goddesses had charm and a sense of humour: traits completely lacking in the Christian, Jewish and Muslim God.

My only anxiety is that if humanity heeded my advice and

reverted to the religion of the ancient Greeks, our generation would completely spoil it. The early Greeks were a pastoral people, their first goddess was Mother Earth and all the later ones originated from, or were connected with, some open-air activity and mother nature. What sort of gods and goddesses would modern humanity worship? The God of the Six-Cylinder Motor Car? Would they pray to the Goddess of Parking? Would they create their own Vestal Virgins to keep alive the Flame of Eternal Tax Evasion? Or have we, perhaps, already reverted to ancient paganism, without noticing it? Are we performing sacrifices on the altars of the God of Television? Are the pop-singers modern pagan gods and nothing else? Or are the Beatles and the Rolling Stones modern versions of ancient Medusa? (Medusa was originally quite good-looking, too.)

And what punishment would a modern Sisyphus or Tantalus suffer? To drive round Hyde Park Corner in a perpetual rush-hour without ever being able to break out of the mad circle of traffic: just to go round and round, forever? Or to stand in never-ending queues for undrinkable cups of tea? To watch Perry Mason every single evening, without the slightest hope that death would ever relieve him?

Another great attraction of the Greek religion was that *things kept happening*. There was always some news on Olympus: that mountain was, in fact, the answer to an ancient gossip-columnist's wildest dreams. There was love, intrigue, unfaithfulness; there were quarrels, escapades, fights, victories and corresponding defeats. Gods had their ups and downs, their status rose or sank; Zeus and Hera started out as equals, but Zeus gradually gained the upper hand. If we revived this ancient religion – as we certainly should – late-night television news-bulletins could bring us: 'The Latest from Olympus'. But nothing ever happens to a modern god – nothing whatsoever. Nothing ever happens in our religious lives, apart from some dull conferences. Miracles – so frequent before they could be properly checked up on – are few and far between nowadays, and when once in a blue moon they do occur, they are so pathetically un-miraculous.

The minor and secondary figures of Greek myth – the extras of religious life – Daedalus, Icarus, the Sphynx, the Centaurs, the Satyrs may be pretty revolting on occasion, but they are interesting and exciting, too; compared with them, our angels and archangels are hopeless bores.

One may remark in objection that not all the myths are attractive. I agree. Some are brutal, even repulsive. No one could stand up for Cronos' devouring his own children – even if this was meant as an allegory. Let's face it – allegory or no allegory – no decent father eats his offspring on any pretext. But even this hardly justified Zeus, his son, in overthrowing his Old Man and keeping him prisoner in a particularly uninviting spot of the Greek hell. You may also feel that many of these myths are also incredible. Can one really believe that Zeus swallowed Metis and afterwards gave birth to Athene through an orifice in his head? This does not sound bloody likely – if I may be permitted to use a literary quote. But I do not think that it taxes one's credulity

'You may be an absolute angel, but you're also a hell of a bore'

more than some other stories about the birth of another God who is happily still with us.

The chief glory of the ancient Greek religion is, however, that it was so human. The Greek gods were incredibly naughty. They took the shapes of goats and other animals to sneak into ladies' bedrooms and then to make love to them (whether they were goddesses, nymphs or ordinary mortal women). They committed adultery and they lied freely; they flew into tempers and were overcome by grief; they were jealous, greedy and mean, but also magnanimous and unselfish: in other words, they were rather like you and me, and our friends. If humanity needs gods, it should create them in its own human image. Modern man commits the grave mistake of imagining himself god-like (in the Biblical sense of the word); the Greeks knew better than this: they turned their deities into warm-hearted, fallible, erring human beings.

And not because they were irresponsible and frivolous, as has often been stated. Think of a monarchy, for example. It is, after all, some sort of modern substitute for Olympus. And the morals of kings and queens have almost always been at variance with the morals of their subjects. An adulterous and gay Henry VIII ruled over a deeply religious, devout England; Edward the Seventh was Prince of Wales during the pompous and self-consciously moral Victorian era; our present cynical, frivolous and rather immoral age is presided over by a simple and sober royal family, the incarnation of all domestic virtues. Similarly, the Greeks were respectable and responsible people, while their Gods were amorous, unreliable cheats and liars, often brutal, always vain. They also fathered innumerable bastards. Olympus – divine or earthly – must be, it seems, the reverse of reality and the incarnation of our dreams. We all live on Olympus, vicariously. If we are sinful, Olympus must be virtuous for all our sins; if we resign ourselves to living a humdrum, bourgeois life, then, at least, our gods and kings must have a gay time. The religious revival I suggest would not only make our lives more colourful, but would make us more virtuous, much to the liking of orthodox morality.

From Ouzo to Feta

I read this wise statement in a travel guide: 'Greece is not a country which you would visit for the sake of the food; but once there, you have to eat.'

I disagree with this. Eating in Greece is far from the painful necessity this remark seems to imply.

Whenever so-called travel specialists come to discuss food, they always explain to the reader that food is a matter of taste. As the particular gentleman, quoted above, put it: 'Whether it is cold or not, is a matter of fact; whether a certain food is good or bad, is a matter of taste.' This is just as silly as most dogmatic statements are. Indeed, it is rather the other way round. In mid-January in Birmingham, an Englishman may exclaim: 'Lovely mild weather we're having!' A visiting Ghanaian or a newly-arrived Pakistani will find the same temperature desperately cold, while any Eskimo who happens to drop in will complain of the heat. So this question of warmth is very much a matter of taste. But concerning food – just as concerning literature – there are absolute standards. A properly prepared French omelette *fines herbes* or a *truite à la Nantaise* is a superb dish, and this is a simple and absolute fact. Mr A. may still not like them; but this will not turn the omelette or trout into a matter of taste. All that has happened is that another fact has emerged: Mr A. does not know what he is talking about.

You may find people – millions of them – who prefer James Bond to *War and Peace*. Yet, it is not a 'matter of taste' whether one prefers Tolstoy to Fleming or *vice versa*.

Another question which almost all writers on Greek food like to dwell on is this: how Greek is it? How European is it, in fact, and – more important – how Turkish? To what extent has it been Hellenized? These analysts remind you of those literary critics who get bogged down trying to trace 'influences' on a writer, while tending to forget the book under review. I do not pretend to know the history of *shish-kebab* and have no idea how *moussaka* developed in the early Middle Ages. But I like them both; if they are primarily a product of Turkey, my congratulations to the Turks.

A Greek meal will probably be preceded by *ouzo*, their aniseed aperitif. It is transparent at first, but when the necessary water is added it turns cloudy. It looks like mouth-wash; it tastes like mouth-wash. The explanation for this is not far to seek: it *is* mouth-wash. In the same breath, I must also warn you against most Greek wine. It is not expensive and usually there is no reason why it should be. And a lot of it is resinated. Resinated wine keeps better; the ancient Greeks resinated their wine, so this is a Hellenic heritage. I personally prefer Homer or Sophocles. Resinated wine is an acquired taste but do not bother to acquire it. People in Greece will advise you to try it with some typical Greek food in a taverna. My advice is, leave it alone. Greek food is excellent; resinated wine spoils it. Leave it to the natives and resident aliens, and stick to the unresinated, which can be quite good.

'Ooouzo!'

On top of all this, resinated wine makes me laugh. Now, I don't mind laughing. I am grateful for a witty remark; I enjoy a scintillating book. But from wine I do not expect the quality of humour. People, as a rule, do not speak often of resin. Why should they? In Hungary, however, we used to mention resin fairly frequently. An old-fashioned gentleman would call out to a gypsy band-leader: 'Come hither and resinate thy bow!' Even this sounds a bit odd to the modern ear; but you just cannot call out to a waiter: 'Come hither, and resinate thy wine!'

Having made these critical remarks, I wish now to put in some powerful words of defence for Greek food. People will make derogatory remarks about it, but Greek food is delicious, particularly if you are prepared for it to be *Greek*. The question is not whether it is better or worse than Swiss, English or Indonesian food: it is different. Their fish and their sea-food are first-class; their baby lamb is a poem; their rich and oily *hors d'œuvre* are unbeatable in their own field; their national dishes, especially *moussaka* and *dolmades*, are not only spicy and tasty, but also *original*. And in Greece you may rediscover the joy of fruit. Eat their grapes, for example, and you will taste the lustre of the vineyard and the warmth of the Mediterranean sunshine in your mouth. And their cheeses! The goat's cheese called *feta* is certainly the greatest contribution Greece has made to human civilization since the time of Menander.

The experts will tell you that in Greece you must eat in absolutely first-class, international restaurants, because elsewhere you cannot be sure of the quality and purity of your food. This is nonsense. Besides, some people cannot afford those absolutely first-class, international restaurants and they, too (as has been rightly pointed out by the gentleman quoted at the beginning of this chapter), have to eat while in Greece. I am no more a devotee of rancid oil than the next fellow; but the risk of your being served with rancid oil is slight, if you use your judgment. In fact, Greece is very much a country where one should visit unfashionable country inns, miles off the beaten track. The Greeks are charming and hospitable people, genuinely interested in you, an exotic foreigner popping up from the back of beyond. If you do not turn up your nose, but show appreciation and interest, the innkeeper will go out of his way to please you.

While the international food experts are busy warning you against small restaurants, in the same breath they are likely to send you off to the *tavernas*. The *taverna* is the Greek equivalent of the French *brasserie* or the Italian *trattoria*, and a very likeable institution it is. In quality they vary from the posh to the filthy, but in all *tavernas* you are expected to go up to the counter – or out to the kitchen – and choose your own food. The *taverna* is a gay place, sometimes a shade gayer than you bargain for. I am not sensitive to noise; in fact, I am the most insensitive man to noise I have ever come across. But in some of these musical *tavernas* I found seven guitarists playing into my ear and the entire *clientèle* howling Thracian and Attic folksongs a little more than I could endure.

Another word of caution – on the subject of Greek hospitality. If you are a tourist, eating in restaurants or on boats cruising between the islands, you eat – more or less – as much as you like. If you find you have too much on your plate, you leave it. More or less, I said, because your waiter or steward – if you are unlucky – may take a personal interest in your welfare and feed you. He will be personally hurt if you leave something on your plate and deeply offended if you do not try those seven or eight novelties he recommends at every meal. And who wants to offend a simple-hearted Greek steward, an unspoilt child of nature? If you are invited to Greek houses (as I often was, and I am in all other respects infinitely grateful for the many kindnesses bestowed upon me) well, then you really must beware of Greek hospitality. It is marvellous; it is generous; it is sincere; it is also deadly. Your hostess will keep recommending various delicacies to you and will not take *no* for an answer. You must taste everything; you must have a proper helping; then a second helping – and enormous helpings, too. And should you refuse a third helping, that will be a clear indication that you hate your hostess's food and mean to insult her and make her a laughing-stock. If you really want to please a Greek housewife, you eat and eat until you turn green and purple; you go on eating until you fall off your chair and die. She will mourn you sincerely because she is sympathetic and gentle-hearted; but that is the only possible way of convincing her that you could not have eaten more.

Meals are eaten at hours which are late for the English, even for the French; Greek meal-times coincide roughly with those in Spain. They lunch at two, even at three, and dine at about ten. After lunch, everybody rushes off to have his siesta. Even the most devastatingly hospitable Greek housewife (should you be her guest for *lunch*) will be extremely keen to see you go. After lunch is siesta-time and the siesta is sacred. You cannot go into a government office after lunch because no one will be there; you will not find any shops open between one and four or four-thirty because the shopkeepers and all their assistants and office-boys are having their siestas; you cannot have your shoes cleaned between two and four because all the innumerable shoe-shine boys are having their siestas.

In the late afternoon, life starts up again. Shops re-open, shoes are shined; government clerks return to their offices at five o'clock – the higher echelon may return at seven or so – and work another couple of hours.

This is not laziness, the Greeks maintain. On the contrary, they will inform you, this habit of breaking the day into two is their main source of energy. It keeps them healthy; it keeps them fit; they sleep less during the night; a maximum of six hours; they can do more and better work than they could without the siesta.

They may be right. Some of the Greek gentlemen I met seemed to be having a pretty leisurely time. But this does not mean that they would not work even less without their siestas.

How to choose a restaurant or a *taverna*? This is one of the tourist's permanent worries. The lists you find in the various guide-books may or may not be reliable. But I found that Athens' taxi-drivers will look after you with a fatherly eye. I got into a taxi with my wife and named a *taverna*.

The driver fell silent and thoughtful. Then he shook his head and said: 'That's rather far and not very good. I'll take you to another which is nearer and better.'

And he did.

Where are they Driving to?

There is no reason why the Greeks should not drive like mad; and they do. Everyone drives as he lives, does everything as he lives, *all* one's actions are manifestations of one's character. Driving, however, releases more hidden energies, stifled passions and frustrated day-dreams than most other activities.

In England, the law-abiding, over-disciplined citizen often becomes a fury: a rude and pushing law-breaker. The French are in a hurry: they live fast and they drive fast. French pedestrians venture out into the open at their own risk, to be hunted as the buffalo used to be in North America. They, too, may soon become extinct. In Italy, the car is even more of a symbol than elsewhere, perhaps because the Italians need more symbols. The Italian car is a toy (it often looks like one); you can make a great deal of noise with it and show off in many wonderful ways. The Greek driver is neither murderous nor rude, nor addicted to law-breaking. But I think a basic trait of the Greek character is a deep, inner insecurity; the Greek needs constant reassurance on all counts. While driving a car, he can reassure himself of his brilliance, quickness of mind and audacity several times a minute. Greek speed and driving tricks are equally dangerous to pedestrians and to other drivers: they have an uncanny tendency to appear from nowhere on the streets of Athens at a speed of sixty miles per hour. But this is incidental;

they are not the mortal enemies of pedestrians and if pedestrians keep away from the roadway, they are only rarely followed onto the pavement or into their homes. The Greek driver wishes to show the world and himself what a clever and skilful fellow he is. He needs little triumphs, tiny victories all the time – cutting in, overtaking, beating the lights – but his instincts are not homicidal, not even particularly aggressive. If, here and there, a few pedestrians escape, he is not really angry and frustrated, as the French driver is.

He is not a law-breaker: at red lights he will pull up (even if with a terrifying screeching of brakes); parking regulations, if not exactly obeyed, are not broken more flagrantly and arrogantly than necessity requires. And even some of their law-breaking is done with true Greek charm and a peculiar sense of fairness. As soon as it starts raining, there is a sudden shortage of taxis in Athens, as in all the other cities of the world. Desperate foreigners stand on the edge of the pavement, forlorn figures, waving at all sorts of vehicles. Then, as likely as not, a private car will pull up and the driver will say: 'I am an auxiliary taxi. Where do you want to go?' The tourist is slightly taken aback, but he is not keen on waiting another forty-five minutes, so he names his hotel. The driver will quote his price, before his passenger gets in. And the extraordinary thing is that, far from taking advantage of the rain and the stranger's plight, he will quote a reasonable price, indeed, considerably less than a taxi would cost. His idea is that this arrangement is fair to all concerned: he wants to make a little money (quite illegally, of course, because he is not a taxi, needless to say, auxiliary or otherwise) but he feels that his fare, too, should share some of the advantages of the transaction.

Whenever we left our hotel in Constitution Square, we came across private drivers, cabbies, lorry-drivers and motorcyclists engaged in lively arguments. They were hardly ever more than that: never really fierce or abusive, never vituperative. Greek drivers argue about certain points of the driving code, matters of right and wrong – they don't just curse and swear at each other. The Greeks' national pastime is (as I have said before) arguing, and the steering wheel is an ideal supplier of raw-material for vociferous, yet basically not too hostile, fracas.

One day, coming home from Sounion, a wing of our car was badly scratched and one of the fenders slightly bent after a brief encounter with a lorry carrying sand. Our driver got out and spent about three-quarters of an hour quarrelling with the lorry-driver, completely ignoring, indeed forgetting, our presence. Most unusual behaviour from a man against whom my only complaint in the past had been that he was too deferential, almost servile. Half the village gathered around us, people took sides, one party supported our driver, the opposing party sided with the lorry-driver. It took me some time to realize that I was witnessing a ritual. Neither cared very much about the damage to his vehicle or the loss of cash; the real point was the damage to their egos and the loss of face. They stayed in the village listening to people, because each driver wanted to hear as often as possible that *he* was not to blame, that it was the *other* fellow who had been driving like a fool. As soon as they had heard often enough what really splendid fellows they were, each a master of his art, they were ready to leave. The motor-car in Greece is a vehicle which is supposed to take you to the haven of self-assurance, the haven of self-confidence and self-esteem, but, alas, on its way there it gets nasty scratches, the fenders are badly bent, and those superficial layers of shiny paint are ruthlessly wiped off.

Sex

Sex-life in Greece is schizophrenic. The female sex is divided into two categories: lewd women who make love for money, and angels – your mother and sisters and, to a much smaller extent, your wife – high above physical desire, active or passive. These two sets of women have nothing in common, except some anatomical affinity, and even that is most regrettable. If you are a lone male in Athens or in other large Greek cities, ponces will not leave you alone: they will make innumerable and most imaginative offers to you, but they would never descend to the level of offering you their sisters. Not even as a joke. One Englishman – remembering his experience in some other lands – tried to make some jocular remarks to a ponce about his (the ponce's) mother and sisters and nearly got a knife between his ribs. (He was rescued miraculously by a waiter whom he had happened to tip generously a short while before.) Another friend, leaving his hotel in Athens at 2 p.m., was accosted by one of these touts. My friend explained that he was not in search of amorous adventure, but of a good steak. He was led to a discreetly lit and sumptuously decorated night-club where a number of seductive (if somewhat superannuated) blondes pounced on him. He turned and fled in a panic, feeling morally outraged: while, as a puritanically minded English businessman, he had nothing against committing adultery, he strongly objected to it in daytime. It just could not be done decently – he felt – before 7.30 p.m. at the very earliest.

Greek prostitutes, by the way, are most efficiently organized; much better, according to some cynics, than the Greek army or the navy. I was informed in Rhodes that whenever the United States Navy paid a courtesy visit to a port, a host of very mobile, migrating prostitutes turned up on the island barely two or three hours after the arrival of the sailors. They came by boat – pleasure cruisers, I presume – but the top bracket prostitutes arrived by chartered flight.

If a girl in Greece is not a prostitute (and, needless to say, comparatively very few are), then she must be a virgin. No half-way houses are permissible. The change in the moral climate is very slow and, so far as it goes, it is a revolution from above. It is the rich girls, with a knowledge of the wide world and with a cosmopolitan outlook, who start placing themselves above oriental, tribal morality and claiming the same freedom for themselves as the males do. These rich and much-travelled girls can set some sort of a fashion and dictate to other circles – to the daughters of the not quite so rich, or the higher echelons of office workers – who are determined not to be left behind or to appear less sophisticated. But the change is slow and is limited to Athens and one or two of the larger cities. In the villages, virginity is still the absolute rule. A girl who is known to have had some sexual experience – however slight and whatever the circumstances – is lost. In some of the more backward places (and about one quarter of Greece is centuries behind those thriving, rapidly developing and changing parts the visitor is likely to see) a strange tradition still persists: after the wedding-night the bridal sheet is exposed to view, to show all and sundry that it bears bloodstains. (In my limited experience – and according to some accounts heard from friends – not all virgins bleed; and *all* non-virgins do occasionally. Besides, plenty of blood can be squeezed out of a girl's fingertips. So, at the present stage of technology, no one fails to put a blood-stained sheet on show. The glorious proof is always there, and if no one else is fooled, the bridegroom always is.)

The question, why should virginity be so highly prized? – is worth examining. The answer is in fact quite simple: in Greece a woman is not quite a *person*; she is a *thing*, a man's property. From a person you may accept behaviour not dissimilar to your own, but newly-bought property should be immaculate. Britain is perhaps the most emancipated country in the world, which does not mean that it is all that emancipated, or that women (or coloured persons or foreigners) are not regarded as inferior by the inferior. But any Briton will be fully aware that his bride may or may not be a virgin on her wedding night and he will not worry unduly. Yet, he would never dream of going into a chain-store and accepting a pair of shop-soiled or second-hand pants as new. He just will not wear a pair of pants if someone else has worn them before him. As regards *persons*, we tend to be tolerant; but goods should be faultless. In Western Europe, a bride is permitted to have lived her own life; but a pair of pants has no life to live and should not have a past. In Greece it is the other way round.

The mother is sacred. Make an offensive – or just a disparaging or sarcastic – remark about a man's mother and he, more likely than not, will knife you. People, literally, get away with murder if they succeed in proving that the victim cursed their mothers. This is a powerful mitigating circumstance which, while it does not excuse murder, certainly reduces it to a minor offence. Mutiny ceases to be mutiny if the recruit has been provoked by remarks uttered by corporal or sergeant throwing doubt on his mother's virtue.

That does not mean that a Greek is always courteous or reverent to his mother. It simply means that he will not tolerate anyone else being disrespectful to her or about her. A Greek mother often rules her son just as a Greek wife often rules her husband: but it is through some device and, more often than not, through *weakness*. Weakness is strength. Tears, sighs, and silent suffering are more effective weapons than shouts and threats. And the weakness of a Greek mother can be pretty powerful.

Mothers – as a second line of defence – try to keep their sons ignorant in sex matters. Sex-education is still practically unknown in Greece, although a breeze of change is beginning gently to blow.

A friend of mine asked a rather revolutionary-minded lady if she thought boys should be given some information about the facts of life. The lady agreed with this, most emphatically, if surprisingly. 'When should they be told?' my friend went on to ask. The lady had no doubts about that either: 'As soon as they have done their military service and come home from the army.'

A woman is still a nuisance in Greece. A girl needs a dowry

Silent suffering

and in most cases her brothers still may not marry before she is safely got out of the way. The dowry is often a heavy obligation and a tremendous sacrifice for the family: it is simply the high price paid to a stranger for ridding the family of a burden. I had a friend – an Austrian – whose uncle, having divorced his wife at the age of fifty after twenty years of marital bliss, was about to marry a girl of twenty. The family remonstrated with him and pointed out: 'Oh yes, this seems to be perfectly all right at present. But you *are* thirty years older, whatever way you look at it. What will happen in twenty years, when you are seventy and your wife only forty?' The bridegroom shuddered with horror: 'You're right!' he said with disgust. 'She'll be forty. Well, I'm afraid, I shall then have to look for a younger wife.'

In Greece the situation is the opposite. Elderly, balding and toothless men marry ravishingly beautiful, teenage girls and then start quarrels with their in-laws about some deficiency in the dowry. No wife has really done her duty to her husband until she has borne him a son, and the wife who bears several daughters without producing a son is regarded as a failure, even as a wicked woman.

All Greeks are brought up in an atmosphere in which women are regarded as inferior. This view includes their wives – but not their mothers. A Greek was asked by a public opinion poll: 'How often do you call the doctor?' He replied: 'For myself, whenever it is necessary. For my mother, every day. For my wife, when she is dying. For my mother-in-law, when she is dead.'

Not all Greeks are quite so articulate; but the mentality

is prevalent. All women are looked down upon *with the exception of the mother*. How is this possible? Well, it is not. Indeed, no Greek can quite rid himself of the suspicion that his mother is in fact a woman. But this notion is unacceptable. It is unbearable. So the mother is turned into a sacred cow, devoid of reality: a worshipped symbol of despised womanhood. You do not *treat* her with any special regard or gentleness, but you draw your knife as soon as she is slighted. At the bottom of your heart you really despise your mother for being a woman, so you have to assail the fellow who echoes those innermost feelings of yours, of which you are afraid and ashamed.

Why, then, this mother-worship? Is there another explanation for it? Let us face it: our love for our mothers is self-love. Her greatest achievement is to have given life to us, thus enriching the world with such a paragon. Whenever I hear extravagant praise of mothers, I am reminded of a biography I once read of Lloyd George. The generous author concluded his endearing Foreword with these words: 'Finally, my thanks are due to Mr Lloyd George, without whose kind co-operation this "Life" would not have been feasible.'

Without our mothers' kind co-operation our lives would not be feasible. And that seems to be the main point in their favour.

There is, of course, an easy way out of this strait-jacket. Give up the idea that everybody else's mother is a fallible and contemptible woman and only yours is an angel and a saint, and there is no more need to draw your dagger the moment someone treats your mother with irreverence. Go on loving your mother, by all means; she most probably deserves it; but you have to accept the idea that other women, too, may be worth-while creatures: sometimes your equals, sometimes inferior to you, but sometimes, alas – let's face the horrible truth – your betters. A sad thought, but an unavoidable one. And that is, after all, not such an easy barrier to jump.

Greek sexual morality and the national Mother Complex is a trap. It is, in fact, a double trap.

The Greeks insist on their girls remaining virgins, so the girls, on the whole, obey. As a result, many boys remain virgins, too; many are sex-starved and frustrated. (More on this problem in the Cyprus chapter.) Decades of hard thinking have driven me to this conclusion: men, on the whole, need women for their sex-life.

There have been many attempts to get round this necessity and to dispense with women; none was truly successful.

Cruising

Greece ought to do well in the mad scramble for tourists. She has a few disadvantages and a certain type of tourist will (and should) avoid her shores. Greece is not a land of night-clubs; she is not a land of casinos. The two casinos, at Corfu and Rhodes, are not only doing badly, but their effect on the visitor is positively somniferous and narcotic.

But the attractions of Greece outshine the few drawbacks: ancient Greece – Olympia, Delphi, the Acropolis of Athens, Delos, etc, etc – are unrivalled in their glory and fascination. The people of Greece are an equal attraction, you cannot help liking them. The islands and the fishing villages are the real Mediterranean at its best. But Greece's most powerful ally is a word.

It is our age which has come fully to realize the power of words. Words can make or mar plans, projects, ideas, political parties, causes. To call a country *backward*, *under-developed* or *developing* is simply using one of three synonyms; yet *backward* carries the stain of a sordid past, *developing* the promise of a splendid future. When a *pilot* is called *captain* and his aeroplane is dubbed a *flagship* our confidence in them increases by leaps and bounds. A *dustman* is a poor dunce of a fellow, but a *refuse-collecting officer* is a man of authority and official glamour. If a *hairdresser* calls himself a *hair stylist* he can charge more; and – conversely – if the phrase *sawbones* had really stuck to our surgeons, they could not possibly dream of charging the fabulous fees of today. *Gallant adventure* and *wallowing in sin and filth* mean exactly the same thing, even if somewhat differently put.

The word which helps Greece is *cruising*. It is a lush word conjuring up all the right associations of luxury and sunshine. It has a tremendous snob-appeal and this is of decisive importance. Travelling in a tramp-steamer from island to island may or may not be much fun; but when the same journey is called *cruising*, it gains lustre. The great firms of chain-stores have created a most effective and welcome revolution by enabling typists and shopgirls to dress like duchesses. The rich, deprived of their distinctive splendour, have to resort to desperate gimmicks to maintain their status. And they have to be pretty imaginative, because last year's trick may seem obsolete today. The poor man's Rolls Royce has arrived, too, and one wonders – not without malicious glee – what next? The popular stores are not selling cheap yachts yet, but no doubt that will come too. In the meantime we have cheap cruising in the Ionian and Aegean seas.

The beauty and charm of ancient Delos or modern Mykonos (just to name two of the popular islands) count for *something*; but the fact that you do not just *go* there, that you do not just *fly* there, that you do not simply *visit* them, counts for much more. They are ports of call on your *cruise*.

The customers of our age may be divided into three groups: (1) There are people who want to get value for their money; or even insist on getting the best at the cheapest possible price. These people make up the customers of

Mrs Elsie Higgs, of 'Fearnlea', Reservoir Road, Edgbaston, on beholding the wonders of Delphi

the famous chain-store empire. (2) There is the group who wants the best, whatever the price. These people go to Knightsbridge shops. (3) There are people who want the most expensive, whatever the quality. They do not complain if what they get turns out to be really good, but that is of secondary importance. Their only requirement is that it should be very, very expensive. Members of this third group are naturally attracted to the Greek islands by the luxuriant, velvety sound of the word *cruise*. Alas, they are often disappointed: there are many reasonable cruises where one gets proper value for money.

The Greek islands have two further great advantages. People love dropping names. Mostly names of other people, of course. Speaking of 'Larry' (as is very fashionable nowadays) when you mean Sir Laurence Olivier, or saying: 'And then I told him: John, you are a scream!' with reference to one of our more distinguished Dukes, is an old but evergreen trick. Dropping names of islands is not quite so good but it enriches one's repertoire. If package tours go to Mytilene, you go to Lesbos, without divulging the fact that the two places are the same. If your neighbour goes to Mykonos (as almost everybody's neighbour does nowadays) you stick to Naxos; if he goes to Chios, you discover Tenos, or, if really hard-pressed, Amorgos. There are so many Greek islands that wherever your neighbour may go, you can always find something not so well-known, smaller and duller.

It is easy to see that a *cruise to Amorgos* is a far cry from a week-end at Eastbourne.

And there is something else we all desire. We all want

to get away from the beaten track. Greece is an ideal country for that, too. It has so many tracks still unbeaten that finding them is child's play. It has never been quite clear to me *why* people should be so anxious to get away from the beaten track, but the desire seems to be universal. I do not like being alone, I am not given to meditation and yoga exercises and I like crowds of people, provided most of them are not standing on my toes and howling into my ears. Why should we hate people so much? On some reflection, it may occur to us – dare I suggest it – that we too are people, almost all of us.

In the following chapters I shall describe three of the large Greek islands: Crete, Cyprus and Rhodes. I know that Cyprus is not a Greek island yet. But in this book Enosis has been achieved. A modest beginning, I admit; but you must begin *somewhere*.

Here I also wish to tell you something of my melancholy visit to a fourth large island, Corfu. When I was a young man in Hungary, I heard a silly joke repeated so often that I cannot help remembering it. A commercial traveller gets a new job and his new boss presents him with his schedule for the first week: 'Monday morning, you are in Bedford [to take English equivalents], early Monday afternoon, at Luton; late Monday afternoon, you reach Birmingham. Early Tuesday morning . . . etc, etc,' for the whole week. When the traveller returns on Saturday morning, the boss enquires: 'Well, how many orders did you get?' The traveller shakes his head in despair: 'Orders? Man, it was as much as I could do to catch all the trains.'

I never thought that one day I would come to re-enact the story of that faded anecdotal hero.

We, my wife and I – were on a cruise – well, we could not resist the word either. Before reaching Corfu, we were told that we would stay five hours on the island. We would have to watch some folk-dancing – all of us: that was compulsory and no excuses – not even a medical certificate – would be accepted. After that, people would have three hours to themselves; various excursions, it was added, could be arranged through the ship's travel bureau.

The lady in charge of the bureau told me privately that a couple who were living in Corfu and were friends of hers, had sent me a special message, saying they would be pleased to show my wife and me round Corfu in their car. We accepted the invitation with pleasure.

Our new friends were waiting for us at the quay-side and came to watch the folk-dancing with us in the Palace which had belonged, in turn, to Queen Elisabeth of Austria and the Kaiser. When the dancing was over, they asked me if I had ever contemplated spending a summer holiday in Corfu. Being a man of impeccable manners I said, yes, very much so (and indeed one can do worse than holiday in Corfu). In that case, my friend declared firmly, he would take me to Corfu's newest hotel, the last word in beauty and luxury, one of the most interesting sights of the island itself and we could make enquiries. Before I could reply, we were shoved into his car and driven across the island for more than an hour. The road ran inland and we saw nothing much of Corfu; he drove like a madman and I – not really a nervous creature – resigned myself to the idea that this

Mrs Elsie Higgs, of 'Fearnlea', Reservoir Road, Edgbaston, on hearing that Delphi was once known as 'the navel of the Earth'

outing was our last journey. At last, we reached the miracle-hotel. Our friend drove into the courtyard and said, without slowing down: 'I'm sorry, but if we stop even for a minute, you'll never catch your boat.' He turned at high speed and drove us back to the port even more furiously than before. He was, by the way, dead right: we just managed to scramble on to our boat at the last minute.

This was, of course, just an average example of Greek hospitality: charming, well-meant, selfless, pointless, reckless and dangerous to life and limb.

The Rugged Island

Flying towards Crete, you will probably remember that, a good while ago, two other travellers flew in this very same airspace: Daedalus and Icarus. Their memory will certainly appeal to your sense of history, if not to your sense of safety.

Having landed and looked around a little, another possible thought may occur to you: Crete is the Texas of Greece. The Cretans are Southerners; they are not the most sophisticated sons of the nation; they are conceited and boastful, but they are also likeable, able and brave; they are convinced that their homeland is the finest spot on earth and its inhabitants are the salt of it. A son of Dallas or Houston will, in all probability, refer to himself as a Texan and not as an American. When I asked a young man here whether he was a Greek or not, he replied proudly, 'Most certainly, I am a hundred per cent Greek.' Then he added, even more loudly, 'And two hundred per cent Cretan.'

But here the parallel ends. Texas is very rich. Crete is very poor. The average annual income of *a family of four* is £300. Here, the equivalent of a halfpenny is certainly still regarded as a respectable sum of money. This is a rough country, the land of long donkey-rides, of mountain-climbing – for other than sporting purposes – and the home of a tough, stern and harsh people.

Herakleion – Iraklion in modern Greek – may confidently compete for the title of the ugliest capital in Europe. Apart from a pretty Venetian fountain, there is not much to look at: neither monuments, nor buildings, nor even the seaside. Its hotels are below the standard of the rest of touristic Greece and its restaurants are below its hotels. We went to dine in Herakleion's best restaurant, accompanied by a Greek friend from Athens. He, too, was regarded as an alien, but not to quite the same extent as my wife and I. So the proprietor – when my friend was discussing our order with him in Greek – said to him: 'Please see to it that the strangers do not catch us out.' These are the terms in which they think: what else could strangers possibly want in Crete except to catch us, the Cretans, out? Life is a struggle at its worst, a game at its best. People are always facing each other from opposing sides and the question is, who catches out the other. When I asked for white grapes and they only had red ones, I caught them out; but when my wife asked for a certain kind of sweet which they did not have either and they succeeded in passing something similar off on us – then they caught us out.

Here we are not far from the Arab lands. The shops are slightly bazaar-like and the shopkeepers try to pull you in – an unheard of practice elsewhere in Greece. When my wife asked the price of a frock, instead of being given a figure, she was asked if she was English or American. The price, obviously, depended on her reply.

Crete is immensely proud of her great sons. Kazantzakis, the eminent writer, was born here (Cretan names usually end with *-akis*) and so was Zeus himself. Quite a few other famous and notorious people, demi-gods and monsters, are associated with the island: Ariadne, Theseus, the above-mentioned Daedalus and Icarus, the Minotaur, and others. Zeus may have been the chief of the Gods, but he is not regarded as the most illustrious son of Crete. The place of honour belongs to Venizelos – the true Chief God of Crete. It was Venizelos who fought for Crete's unity with Greece – a struggle for a large island which ended in Enosis in 1913, but which has recently been overshadowed by the struggle of another Greek island. Venizelos started as a local Cretan politician and was largely responsible for the exchange of populations which rid Crete of her Turkish minority and thus of a grave and uncomfortable problem. Crete still follows in Venizelos's political footsteps, vaguely conceived and re-interpreted today. But Venizelos's true greatness did not consist in bringing about Crete's unity with Greece; or in his successes in the Balkan wars; or in getting rid of the Turks; or in the brilliance or validity of his policies. His true greatness lay in his being a Cretan.

Much of what I have said seems to be critical of the Cretans. But Crete is certainly one part of Greece which no visitor should miss. More and more people go there every year and still more and more should. There are four main reasons for visiting the island.

(1) In all fairness, if Herakleion is not very beautiful, the island itself is. If Herakleion is not rich in international luxury hotels, St Nicolas has a luxury bungalow site which is about as good as the Mediterranean can offer anywhere. Crete is developing fast and is catching up. If I were a property-

speculator (which, alas, I am not) I should put a lot of my money in Cretan sites.

Crete also has a very nice climate: the swallows of Crete stay put and refuse to migrate. It's not that they are lazy or stick-in-the-mud types. They just find Crete pleasant and warm.

(2) The greatest attractions, however, are the remains of Minoan culture at Knossos. Libraries have been written about the most ancient European civilization, of Schliemann's hunch, Evans' excavations, and there is not much point in repeating any of it here. This is one story which makes one proud of humanity; it is also a detective – or adventure – story (particularly if coupled with the story of Troy) with few rivals. The Palace of King Minos (or rather, many King Minoses) is one of the most exciting and exhilarating sights of the ancient world, and Phaestos is a good second to it. King Minos's palace had its own system of flush-lavatories and they seem to have worked better than the flushing system of an average, present day hotel in Herakleion. The museum in the capital is breath-taking; I am choosing my words carefully. I am no lover of museums and my breath needs quite a lot of taking.

(3) Crete is extremely cheap, too. If someone is no sybarite, not a soft and pampered son of the affluent society, like myself, and does not mind roughing it a bit, he will find Crete a paradise. A main dish in the best restaurant may not cost more than two shillings; a room for a night in a peasant house may be found for four or five shillings; and one can live much cheaper even than that. I met a slightly eccentric Englishman who spends several months in Crete every year and his monthly expenditure is £4.

Master Timothy Winterbottom, of Abbas Manor Preparatory School, Bath, on hearing that he is to be shown the remains of Minoan culture at Knossos

(4) One of Crete's greatest charms is her people. History – Venetian and Turkish occupation – made them tough; the ruggedness of their country made them poor. We all – those of us, who are old enough – remember the great Battle of Crete in World War II and the subsequent heroic stand of the Cretans against the Germans. The *Ill-Met By Moonlight* episode, the kidnapping of the German General Kreipe, was one of the outstanding cloak-and-dagger stories of the war. (I asked a member of the Herakleion town council why the spot where the General was captured – and which I visited – was not marked by a commemorative sign and I received the surprising reply, 'We thought that German tourists might not like it'.)

The Cretans are a stern and slightly humourless people, who take their pleasures seriously and dutifully. A proper Cretan wedding takes about five days, as long as a Test Match, provided of course that the guests are not bowled out prematurely. Cretan kindness, hospitality and simplicity, however, are unique reminders of the Unspoilt Man of the pre-Touristic Age. With a Cretan gentleman, I made a car journey round the island. On our way back to Herakleion, we stopped at the tiny village of Chourmedzion. Forewarned of the famous Cretan hospitality, I did my best to avoid it. These people, I knew, were extremely poor. I did not want to be a burden to them and told the President of the village that I could not stay more than ten minutes. Surely, he asked me, I would take some refreshment with them. Yes, I would, with pleasure, I replied. To refuse would have meant a grave insult; and perhaps a small-size penknife in my ribs.

In no time there was *raki* – their rough but tasty version of brandy – and cheese and nuts on the table, later followed by wine. Within a quarter of an hour three hundred people – the entire male population of the village – had surrounded us, showing real, if puzzled, delight in seeing me. I had honoured their village with my visit, they said, and when I replied, quite moved, that on the contrary, it was they who were honouring me, they laughed heartily, as if I had said something incredibly amusing. An hour later I made another attempt to leave, repeating my apologies and excuses and expressing my sincere thanks, when the President and the Priest informed me that it was impossible to depart just now: the dances were just about to begin and, besides, supper was almost ready.

Some village musicians came forward with their guitars and started playing monotonous but rhythmical and quite charming Cretan songs and three men began to dance: two middle-aged peasants and a youth of about eighteen. There was nothing comical in this trio: they were loveable and dignified and they danced well. Then some others brought in huge lamb chops grilled on charcoal – the hospitality of people who rarely eat meat themselves. They gave me a sharp Cretan knife – a murder-weapon, if I ever handled one – but they advised me not to use it. 'Here in Crete,' a man remarked, 'we say that women and meat should always be touched by hand.'

Then, about five hours after my arrival, a terrifying thought occurred to me and I asked them what they thought of tourism and its prospects. They fell silent and became thoughtful. Yes, they knew that more and more tourists were visiting Greece and they were hoping that many of them would come to their village, too. But would they offer the same hospitality to all? Yes, they certainly would do their best to please people who honoured their village by visiting it. One village elder was doubtful.

'Oh yes, tourism . . .' he repeated with a sigh.

The others, obviously knowing what he was about to say, tried to shut him up but could not. If a Cretan wants to say something, he will say it: 'We like tourists. But we cannot afford them.'

'Afford them?' I asked, feigning surprise, but by now, of course, I knew what he meant.

'No, we can't,' the old man went on sadly. 'They will ruin us. We can afford a few tourists, but not a flood.'

These people were absolutely determined to treat all tourists as guests. There was no question of accepting money from the tourists. To accept money from guests was contemptible.

I told them that they must grow up and accept the facts of life. Tourism is a world-industry and had made other countries rich. They may please the tourists in many other ways, but they must also accept payment from them.

'We can't possibly do that,' they protested. 'A guest is a guest, whatever he calls himself. If they honour our island and our village by visiting us, they must be properly treated.'

One of them produced a new argument: 'I really do it out of selfishness. When a villager comes here, he is offered hospitality and food and shelter for the night. But when I find myself stranded in a strange village, I too, can be sure they will treat me the same way.'

'By all means,' I nodded. 'But would you treat foreign tourists in the same fashion?'

'Of course, we would,' the whole village chanted, hurt by the question.

'But you must not do that,' I went on. 'Go on being hospitable to Cretans and other villagers, but Americans and Englishmen and others can afford to pay and, in fact, prefer to pay. Besides, you're in for a surprise if you expect hospitality in return from them. You could jolly well starve in the gutter in New York or London and no one would turn a hair.'

Those with a little knowledge of the world knew that I was right.

'All the same,' they said, 'it just goes against the grain to accept money from tourists.'

The village elder agreed with them heartily. He said, 'No, mister, you are wrong here. Money just should not enter into tourism.'

The Troubled Island

It's all peace and quiet and sheer luxury in the swimming pool of the Ledra Palace Hotel in Nicosia. The hot, Middle-Eastern sun shines brightly on the dark-blue water; sun-tanned bodies loll on the comfortable, super-elegant deck-chairs; discreetly but incessantly, the stereo-loudspeakers pour out Greek pop songs. Go to the bar or sit down at one of the tables by the water, or just ring the bell (I personally hate ringing bells) and unsmiling but polite waiters will bring you cool drinks and double-decker sandwiches. It is true that on the way down you noticed United Nations soldiers in the corridors of every floor of the hotel. Young men, sitting under reading lamps, turning the pages of Danish glossy magazines with innumerable pictures of alluring bosoms and other interesting parts of the female anatomy – a glass of iced orangeade on their right, a light machine-gun on their left. It is also true that most of those sun-burned young men, diving into the water from the highest springboard or throwing furtive – and, you are pleased to notice, admiring – glances at your wife, are officers of the United Nations peace-keeping force. Swimming on your back and looking up, you notice other blue-beretted U.N. soldiers on the roof of the Ledra Palace: they watch you, sweating under the hot sun and wishing, no doubt, that *they* were down in the cool water and *you* up on the sizzling roof-top. You listen to the muffled thud of tennis balls from the neighbouring court and you know that this time it is neither mad dogs nor Englishmen who are playing tennis in the midday sun, but two Finnish officers who, new arrivals, cannot yet tell the difference between 'lovely weather' and tropical heat.

'This Paradise may turn into a blazing inferno at any moment,' you tell yourself a little melodramatically, using the language of tabloid journalism in order to ease your conscience. But you know it may not – you know it will not. A U.N. debate is imminent and both sides are on their best behaviour – so you and your wife are as safe as the young soldiers on the roof-top.

You are safe in another respect, too. Here in the water they leave you alone. But you are well aware that outside there are six hundred thousand Cypriots – 82 per cent Greeks and 18 per cent Turks – who are *all* eager and determined to explain the Cyprus problem to you. You close your eyes and shudder in the sunshine: you know there is no getting away from them. They *will* explain it to you. And it is a pity, you feel; of course you really came here to find out about the 'situation'; but when you came you thought you knew *something* about it and felt that basically it was all very simple and you could solve it in a quarter of an hour. Since then you have listened to complicated details, bewildering statistics, interminable statements, articles of the constitution, the grievous wrongs committed by the other side, and the Cyprus problem has become elusive, cloudy and intimidating.

Looking left as you leave the hotel, you see sandbags and

notice that some of the walls are chipped by rifle bullets. If you turn left, you cross the Green Line, and a few steps take you into the Turkish quarter, with all its misery, semi-starvation, lack of petrol and traffic at a standstill; with men sitting in cafés all day long because they have nothing better to do, and children playing in the filth; but you – or rather your car – will turn right, into the rich and elegant Greek section, with its bustling traffic, sports competitions, Russian film week, gaiety and busy tumult. 'Poor Turks,' you are inclined to say because you are a soft Westener, known to be of good will, always ready to stick up for the underdog of the moment. But no problem is quite as simple as that: you have to dive deep into it, from the highest spring-board, like the sun-tanned, athletic U.N. officers diving into the water of the Ledra Palace Hotel swimming pool.

Before you come to realize that what seemed so simple is, indeed, as simple as it looked, you have a long and devious way to travel. First of all, you have to find the answer to a few basic questions: *Who* are these people, the *dramatis personae*, involved in it all? Then: *Where* are you? And: *What* is it all about?

Well, who are they? You know, of course, that the people of Cyprus are Cypriots. Not Greeks living in Cyprus; not Turks living in Cyprus, but Greek and Turkish Cypriots. Through usage, this terminology has long ago lost its comic undertone. We do not speak of Chinese Singaporians and Malay Singaporians, or French Guernsians and English Guernsians, but the Greeks and Turks of Cyprus must be called Greek or Turkish Cypriots. The difference between the two is that one nationality speaks bad Greek, the other speaks bad Turkish. Otherwise there is no difference. Oh yes, we know that the Turks are poorer, less well educated, and so on. I also know that some people claim they can look at a man and tell for certain whether he is a Turkish or a Greek Cypriot. But this is utter nonsense. There are, of course, certain typical Turkish faces and some typical Greek faces, and sometimes it may be possible to tell. But in most cases you cannot. I would not dare to say what I am saying less than a thousand miles away from Cyprus. U.N. debate or no U.N. debate, both the Turks and the Greeks would shoot me in the back for it.

The Greek Cypriots lack a great deal of the charm, sense of humour and natural gaiety of the mainland Greeks. They are less serene, more sullen, and take themselves much more seriously. They are not really Greeks: they *are* Cypriots, after all, resembling the Turks of this island rather than the Greeks of the mainland. The truth remains, that there is not much difference between the two: they are the sons of the same island, the same climate, the same strife.

If the Cypriots are neither very Greek nor very Turkish, they certainly are rather English. Britain occupied the island for eighty-two years and her influence is ubiquitous. Cars still travel on the left-hand side of the road and there is bread-and-butter pudding on the menu of the Ledra Palace. The administration is better and smoother than in Greece, the standard of living higher. Many people speak English – so the Cypriots are more articulate *vis-à-vis* the world at large than one would normally expect from such a small island. Cypriots keep English hours: there is no siesta here, as on the mainland and no return to the offices at five o'clock for a further two or three hours; in Cyprus they tried this out, but reversed to their good old English habit of working from 9.30 a.m. to 5.30 p.m., with a one-hour break for lunch.

As in so many former colonies, the grudging respect felt for the English has given way to a feeling of affection, almost of love. This is surprising, and no one was more surprised by it than the Cypriots themselves. More than eighty years of co-existence and about a decade of mutual murder creates a feeling of intimacy. 'Yes, I used to love the English,' an influential Cypriot lady told me, 'but I shall never forgive them for their attitude in the present quarrel. Not because it is what it is; but because it makes it utterly impossible for me to go on loving them.'

The fourth layer of the population is the U.N. Force. The Greeks used to be annoyed with them and called them 'Tourists'! This, for some mysterious reason, was felt to be a grave insult and the U.N. took it as such. Today, it is generally recognized that they are doing a good job by keeping the two sides apart. They are not empowered to *do* much more and their commanders – with a great deal of understanding and with infinite patience – try to reason with people and keep the *status quo*. No new fortified positions are to be built, and each side is supposed to keep to its present territory. The Greeks are well-off, the Turks are poor; the Greeks lack nothing, the Turks are in need of almost everything. So the U.N. soldiers feel sympathy for the Turks and help them with little gifts – consequently the Greeks regard them as pro-Turkish and biased. But a Swedish private from Malmo, who gives a small, hungry Turkish child a piece of chocolate, is not expressing a well-considered political attitude. He is simply giving a small child a piece of chocolate.

The U.N. boys are mostly volunteers: they come for six months and get very good pay. They do their job and remain completely uninvolved in the political situation. They could not care less who is right and who is wrong: it is none of their business. They are decent young men, mostly from the North (north of Europe, like the Swedes, Danes and Finns, or the north of America, like the Canadians), they wish they could have more sweets for little Turks and they are also terribly sex-starved. Cyprus is a place where virginity is at a premium (as everywhere in Greece or Turkey) and Cypriot girls will not even sit with U.N. soldiers in cafés or go with them to the cinema. The soldiers often live in primitive circumstances – at the back of beyond – sometimes they find it difficult to wash properly, but they do their duty good-naturedly, have their wages paid into their bank accounts at home, remember that six months is not a very long time, and are terribly glad that they do not have to understand the Cyprus problem. (Except, of course, that the Irish and the Canadians are instinctively anti-partition.)

The second question you ask yourself is: where is Cyprus? You should not have to wonder: Cyprus is in the Middle East. Not only because the climate is much hotter than that of the Greek mainland; not only because the Lebanon is just over a hundred miles away and the rugged coast of Asia Minor less than half that distance; but because the people's mentality is Eastern. The 1960 solution – the creation of the Cypriot state – failed because it was a compromise solution, and compromise, the very idea of give-and-take, the *quid pro quo*, is as strange to the Middle-Eastern mind as a murderous family vendetta would be to Yorkshire farmers. In Cyprus the other side is always base, mean and treacherous in *everything*, from beginning to end, while you yourself are always noble and generous, a knight in shining armour. General Grivas, looking back over his EOKA career, found – and said so repeatedly – that he had been right in everything he had done. He had not made one single mistake, not even in minor matters. You might find it strange – he remarked in his book – that one man should always be right but, strange as it might appear, that was the case. He had, however, an explanation to offer: he must have been guided by providence. He must indeed. All Cypriots always are: providence, God, Allah – the name may vary, but the fact remains that they are always right.

The Cypriot press is the press of the Middle East. It is scurrilous, libellous and utterly unreliable; it is also flamboyant, vituperative and boastful. The 'murderers of the Cypriot nations'; the 'madmen of NATO'; the 'imperialist monsters'; 'scandalmongers and intriguers'; 'only the British and their agents stand to gain from bloodshed . . .' etc, etc – such phrases are among their more moderate utterances.

It is interesting to find that political dirt is always mingled with a fair amount of sexual dirt. One day, the Turkish press of Nicosia reported that Greek guardsmen had been found in a compromising and unnatural situation in the bushes of the Presidential palace. The scandal was, of course, hushed up and no one heard about it except the Turkish

General Grivas

jornalist. As a reply to this, *Elevtheria* reported that a 'Turkish family which had escaped from the hold of Turkish terrorists and sought protection from the Cyprus government' (as far as one knows, no such families really exist) 'declared that the Turkish rebels have sunk so low as to rape even school-girls'. The implication being, I suppose, that until then only girls over school-leaving age had been raped. On another occasion the Greek Cypriot press reported that the British had imported fifty 'dancing girls' to undermine and corrupt the morals of the Cyprus government and senior Civil Servants. No one takes these reports seriously or pretends that there is even a grain of truth in them. They are not even rumours: they are meant as entertaining titbits of no consequence. People read them, nod with satisfaction – perhaps smile with faint pleasure – and turn their attention to other matters.

You cannot find out from Cyprus newspapers what is happening in the world. There may or may not be a brief summary of world events but, as a rule, almost the entire newspaper will deal with Cyprus affairs as though Cyprus were the centre of the universe. And, of course *it is*. That is the main point you have to grasp. When you wonder *where* you are, the answer is: you are at the centre of the world. When Khrushchev – in the last days of his power – talked about the terrifying weapons Russia possessed, the only meaning of this – according to the Cyprus press – was that Cyprus was safe. After this, the imperialist monsters would be intimidated and Cyprus could rejoice. Every world event, every declaration made by every world politician has a bearing on Cyprus and it depends on Cyprus –

and Cyprus alone – whether the world is to live in peace or to go to war. And this, you realize, has become the dividing line – the true Green Line – momentarily, at least – between Turkish and Greek Cypriots. The Turks – isolated and hungry – are passionately interested in food, water supplies, bread, work, petrol and fuel; the Greeks in world politics, war, peace, international treaties, pacts with Great Powers, and the fate of humanity, which last is to be decided as a side-issue of the Cyprus question. The Cypriots know that they cannot become a World Power; but they have succeeded in becoming a World Nuisance, which is almost as good.

Being a simple soul, you probably thought that Cyprus was an overwhelmingly Greek island so, sooner or later, it should go to Greece. That's how the problem looked to Winston Churchill, who visited the island in 1907. 'I think it is only natural,' he wrote, 'that the Cypriot people of Greek descent should regard their incorporation, with what they call their mother-country, as an ideal to be earnestly, devoutly and fervently cherished. Such a feeling is an example of the patriotic devotion which so nobly characterizes the Greek nation.' Great Britain actually offered Cyprus to Greece in 1915, as the price for Greece's joining the Allies. The Greeks – or rather their king – hesitated; when they did eventually join, it was too late: the Cyprus offer had lapsed. Yet, I have always thought and still think: Cyprus is a Greek island, so – after giving the necessary safeguards to the minority – it should become a part of Greece, like Rhodes, Crete, Chios, and other islands in those regions.

However, as soon as the Greek Cypriots begin to elaborate on the justice of their cause, you start to feel doubtful. They will tell you that it was under duress that they signed the 1960 Zurich and London agreement, which is nonsense; they signed it as free agents and they were free not to sign it. You have the feeling that they accepted the benefits of that treaty and are now trying to get out of their obligations. The treaty does not work, they continue, *consequently* it is not valid; it has become null and void. What a simple way – you murmur – to get out of treaty obligations: as soon as there is a dispute, the treaty becomes null and void.

The treaty is certainly not null and void, but it was awkward and absurd. It guaranteed a certain quota of Turks in the Civil Service; it was not simply a question of finding the right person for the right post, the main thing was that he had to be a Turk. When it turned out that there was a shortage of literate Turks, Dr Kutchuk insisted that Turks ought to be imported from the mainland rather than have Greek Cypriots appointed. Besides, the constitution, in an attempt to perpetuate itself, declared that it must not be changed. Never. No majority, even two hundred years later, could be enough to change one single comma of it. The Turks insisted on every letter of the constitution, while the Greeks, with Makarios in the lead, never missed a chance to show that they held the Turks in rather low esteem. The Turks refused to vote for an income-tax law because, in their interpretation of the constitution, a definite part of the income tax ought to be devoted to the benefit of the Turks alone. Dr Kutchuk had the veto in several important matters and could cripple the administration. Municipalities came to a standstill, too, because this or that rigid rule of the constitution proved unworkable. Makarios suggested a revision of the constitution, a suggestion which – thanks to the idiocy of the constitution – seemed itself a breach of the constitution. This triggered off civil war between the two communities – no one really knows exactly how it started. This is all true; yet, when you begin to listen to the Turkish argument, you feel that the Greeks might, after all, be right.

They say that Greeks and Turks can *never* live amicably side by side, so partition is the only solution. But minorities live in peace – well, often not in peace, but they *live*, side by side – all over the world. Hungarians live in Rumania, Finns in the Soviet Union, Chinese in Malaysia, Indians in the West Indies, etc, etc. They can all live together – but Turks and Greeks cannot. Of course, they *do* live together, in Istanbul, and Rhodes, and Western Thrace; but they cannot possibly live together in Cyprus. But if partition were the only solution for the minority problem, the whole world would disintegrate into infinitesimal communities. The Turks also say that Cyprus – united to Greece – would be a threat; a dagger aimed at the heart of Turkey. But there are other Greek islands, nearer to Turkey, and they cause no trouble; and is no threat implicit in the long land-frontier between Turkey and Greece? On top of all this, Greece and Turkey are allies – and, apart from Cyprus they do not have much to quarrel about just now – so why should a Cyprus, united to Greece, be a threat to an ally?

The trouble is that there is not one Cyprus question but

many. Or perhaps there isn't even one. Greece wants Enosis, unity with Cyprus, and Turkey wants partition – and as far as the world knows, this is the Cyprus problem. But it is not. Britain wants bases to guard her route to the Persian Gulf. America prefers the staunch, reliable, anti-Communist Turks to the fickle Greeks. (Fickle Greece fought on the Allied side in two world wars; reliable Turkey fought against them in the first and remained neutral in the second.) Russia wants a foothold in the Mediterranean and knows that it is easier to undermine Cyprus than Greece. Nasser uses the Cyprus troubles as a lever for getting rid of some British bases in the Mediterranean. Turkey does not really care quite so much for her hundred thousand people in Cyprus as it seems. They used to say so, quite openly, not so long ago. There are many more Turks in Bulgaria or in the Soviet Union, who are never even mentioned. But she is in an awkward situation, under grave internal pressure. We had a saying in Hungarian: 'I've caught a Turk and now he won't let me go'. Turkey has caught a hundred thousand Turks (or Turkish Cypriots) and they won't let her go. The Greek Cypriots – as I have already pointed out – are more interested in bullying the world and reminding it of their own importance than in Enosis – so the Cyprus problem is really buried under its own side-issues. Only the Greeks on the mainland seem to remember how it began – and they are terribly out-of-date.

The world is shrinking: units become larger and larger. Continental countries embrace one another with some reluctance and form the Common Market and EFTA, and it takes less than four hours to cross the Atlantic. Yet, all the time, tinier and tinier states are being born. Malta becomes a nation. Cyprus becomes a nation. And as though Cyprus were not small enough as it is, we are told that she must be divided up still further.

Cypriots talk of 'unrestricted independence'. Great Britain listens to them wistfully. How nice it would be for Britain to achieve unrestricted independence. A dream Britain gave up long ago. But not Cyprus.

Cyprus, in a way, has achieved *all* her aims, however contradictory. Greeks and Turks do live amicably together on the island: in Limassol, for example, the Turks were defeated, so there is no dividing line, no Green Line between the communities. The same situation prevails in a few villages. In these places, everyone watches the Turks moving about and living among Greeks as though it were a miracle; as though it had not been the normal situation for centuries.

But Cyprus has also achieved partition. The island is, to all intents and purposes, divided into a Turkish part and a Greek part. The Green Line is a challenge to everyone. Diplomats, soldiers and journalists may cross it freely. But any ordinary Greek or Turkish Cypriot would probably be shot or at least arrested if he ventured across. So everyone longs to cross it. The Turks are cut off from the sea in most of their areas, so their longing for the world at large is more rational. Nicosia is a divided city, like Berlin or Jerusalem; many Greek Cypriots are tormented by the desire – or at least the itch – to cross the Line, simply because the Line is there. People are like that. I am sure Adam did not really like apples at all.

Many Cypriots long, at the same time, to return to normalcy. It is nice to be at the centre of world interest, but you can have too much of a good thing. 'We want tourists again,' a Cypriot politician told me. 'I really don't know why they've stopped coming. It's very quiet here now, isn't it?'

An American friend, a writer of travel-books, nodded seriously.

'I'm sure you are right,' he said. 'People are fond of adventure, and Americans like it more than other people. It's all a question of angling your advertisement. You could turn it into a challenge. Why not say, for example: "ARE YOU BRAVE ENOUGH TO COME TO CYPRUS?" Or perhaps it might appeal to Texans if you said: "COME TO CYPRUS AND SHOOT IT OUT!" You may add: "JOIN ANY SIDE YOU LIKE." '

There is one dreaded moment in the life of all dreamers: the moment when their dreams come true. It's wonderful to cherish a grudge and to fight for an ideal. But what happens when the grudge disappears or the ideal is achieved? Such a turn of events has been the source of endless disappointments, even tragedies.

The Cypriots are in grave danger. World public opinion is slowly coming round and people have begun to say what they ought to have been saying from a long time: why should a Greek island be prevented from becoming a Greek island? Enosis is on the horizon (vaguely and dimly as yet) but even this is a grim warning to many Greek Cypriots.

A number of Greek Cypriots still want Enosis. Grivas

still wants it. Some of his National Guardsmen still want it. But the Communists – a formidable proportion of the Cyprus population – do not want it. Their brief is not to join a NATO power, nor to increase the strength of the Atlantic Alliance. And why should they be so keen on joining a country where the Communist Party is banned, while in Cyprus it is free? Russia wants a foothold in the Eastern Mediterranean, not a NATO base in a Greek Cyprus.

Extreme right – as so often happens – joins hands with extreme left. Many of the big capitalists of Cyprus do not find the prospect of becoming part of Greece any too attractive. The standard of living is higher in Cyprus than it is in Greece. The Cyprus pound is a better currency than the drachma. The Civil Service is more efficient than in Greece. And the people – not speaking of the politicians – have got used to being the centre of the universe. Cyprus is an independent state, a member of the U.N., a factor in international politics: is it really such an attraction to become a province of Greece? Makarios is President of an independent state; does he really want to become archbishop of a small island? He says he does. He said so to me. Otherwise he speaks of 'unrestricted independence' only; once that is achieved, Cyprus will decide what to do. Of course, I do not doubt the President's word, but I'm sure many of his ministers and Civil Servants do not share His Beatitude's nobility of spirit, and having been potentates of a famous little country, they are not keen on becoming insignificant, provincial bureaucrats. There are signs of tension between Greece and Cyprus; even minor signs of friction. The Cypriots resent the alleged interference of Greek army officers with the running of the National Guard; one Greek diplomat has even been expelled from Cyprus; and while Greece was canvassing support in the West, stating that a Greek Cyprus would be a gain for NATO, President Makarios was gaily proclaiming that the dismantling of *all* military bases is a *condition* of Enosis.

While talking to the Archbishop of the present problems, I recalled the struggle for Enosis of another large Greek island, Crete. That successful struggle was led by another politician who also became a national hero of Greece, just like Archbishop Makarios. That other politician eventually became Premier of Greece and is nowadays generally recognized as the greatest statesman Greece has ever produced. His name was Venizelos. Listening to Archbishop Makarios, I wondered whether *he* ever remembered this story. And if he did, whether it ever occurred to him that SISONE might be a practical programme. This is, of course, the reverse of ENOSIS. Why not attach Greece to Cyprus? Not as a colony of course; but as a union of free nations? It would be so much easier. And in Cyprus one has the occasional feeling that it would be more justifiable, too.

And this leads us to put the question: what is really behind this unique and curious Cyprus question? Why did it become a question at all? Was it really necessary?

Some called the Eoka fighters terrorists, others called them heroes. They massacred innocent citizens and, in turn, were hanged, sometimes just for possessing firearms. Leaving the moral judgment aside, one has the awful feeling that the whole Eoka struggle was a little pointless. They would

His Beatitude

have achieved independence without it. Malta became independent without an Eoka – indeed, without one single bomb being exploded. And scores of other countries, too. Why, oh why, did Eoka occur in Cyprus, of all places?

I do not know the answer. But I have a vague suspicion. I said before, that the world has already forgotten about the comic undertones of the word *Cypriot*. The world may have; the Cypriots have not. They know that they are neither fish nor fowl; neither Europeans nor people of the real Middle East; neither Greeks nor Turks. They are Cypriots. Turkish and Greek Cypriots, are alike; in fact, they are indistinguishable from one another – their mortal enemies. They are people in search of their true identity. Such a search always has an element of despair in it; sometimes an element of schizophrenia. A man, in search of his true self, may easily become violent. Because he can never, never find what he is looking for.

Perhaps sexual starvation plays a part in it, too. I have already mentioned that in the Cypriot press political obscenity is often mingled with sexual obscenity. Nothing is more natural. A gun can, after all, be a sexual organ. A poor one – but still a sexual organ. Mods and Rockers throw fireworks around on Margate beach; others throw bombs in Cyprus. One cannot help feeling that had the Cypriot girls been just a shade less virtuous, the history of Cyprus would be less eventful and much happier.

With such thoughts on your mind, you set out for another tour of Nicosia. You are a journalist, so you cross over into the Turkish quarter. U.N. officers are your guides and they know all the Turks – who are poor, often in rags, often hungry, often barefooted. They show you spots where wicked Greeks killed Turkish children, but you know that wicked Turks in turn killed Greek children – so this particular account is more or less balanced. All Greek notices – to the last letter – have disappeared; it's Turkey now. Everywhere you see pictures of Makarios on the walls – complete with horns and hooves. You are in luck today: a Turkish taxi happens to have a drop of petrol and is ready to take you to the village of Mandres Hamit, sixteen kilometres away. It used to be a village of two hundred souls; now it has become a tent-town of 3,500 inhabitants. They are all Turkish refugees from a nearby village called Omorphita, and they all live in tents in indescribable filth, without proper sanitation, without proper food. There is nothing they can – or will – do all day except sit around and gape at each other. They have lost their jobs – they can't get out, in any case. They have no medical attention and the first school for their five hundred children is yet to open. Tomorrow. Or the day after tomorrow.

The place is a sink of filth and squalor, poverty and hopelessness. They cook on paraffin stoves. They have no electricity; indeed, they have no lighting of any sort, and when darkness falls, it means complete darkness in Mandres Hamit. The sun is still shining brightly, but winter is approaching slowly and you know that these people have little hope. Your political sympathies may be with the Greeks; your human sympathies are with the Turks; not because they are more virtuous; simply because they need it more. The

Turks can actually *see* their former dwelling places from here, but the Greeks will not let them go back to their looted and half-destroyed village three miles away because these people are not people but a means to put pressure on the Turks and teach them a lesson. They are 'traitors' and have only got their deserts. That, of course, includes the children under five. The Turks will not help these unhappy people either, because they are not people but a means to show the world how cruel, barbarous and heartless the Greeks really are. You thought, when you were young and innocent, that politics was about *people*. But you were very, very wrong. The Cyprus question is, in fact, heading towards a much-dreaded, successful solution, while people of Cyprus are rotting away in tents. You drive back to the bar of your luxury hotel on the Greek side, order a gin and tonic, discuss Russian pressure, or the rumoured rift between Makarios and Grivas, but you cannot forget that little Turkish boy of four who looked at you with his huge, black eyes and shouted an impish 'hallo' to you, and who, you know, will go to sleep tonight with ten other people in a dark, stinking tent. But you are a fool. You ought to think in terms of diplomatic notes and bases and Communist pressure and NATO and not in terms of little children.

The Borrowed Island

'This is a gentle island; a friendly island, because we are not war-like people at all. Warring is silly and pointless. We are kind and mild.' It was an old Rhodian Greek who spoke. This was no boasting; nor was he on the defensive. He was stating facts.

'Ours is a lovely island; so lovely that quite a few people have taken the trouble to occupy it: the Knights of St John, the Turks, the Italians. We always tried to come to terms with everybody. For example, we said to the Turks: "Leave us alone as much as you possibly can. You are the occupying power: all right, we are quite willing to pay you an annual ransom. But let us carry on with our trade and let us lead a normal life. You needn't keep a large garrison here, that would be very expensive and an utter waste. We are not going to rebel. Naturally, you will have to keep a police force here and we shall pay for *that* in our ransom." We struck a bargain along those lines and we did not have much trouble with the Turks.'

'What about the Italians?' I asked.

'We never quarrelled with the Italians either. Perhaps even less than with the Turks. In fact, we got on with the Italians extremely well. They took a lot of pride in Rhodes and were determined to turn it into a popular holiday resort – in which they succeeded. I am a Greek and a good

Greek too, but there is no denying that the Italians did a great deal for Rhodes. They had a mania for building – alas, often in the pompous, ostentatious Mussolini style – but they built many good, useful things, too. At the end of the war, the Italians, being very intelligent people, fully realized that the game was up and they had to clear out. They did not argue and did not bargain: the new régime realized that the Fascists had done great harm to Greece and handed over Rhodes with good grace. Thus they laid the foundation stone of a future good relationship, which we have today. We parted as friends and the Italians love coming back to Rhodes for holidays. It's "abroad" for them; yet many of us speak their language; besides, the place is cheap; and it is still their beloved Mediterranean.'

'And how did the Turkish minority behave under Italian rule?'

'Perfectly well. We had no trouble with the Turks. When the Italians left, there were no vendettas between Greeks and Turks. We lived together in peace; we go on living together in peace.'

This was a very different story, and a very different mentality, from that of Crete and Cyprus. I heard that an official organization was planning to publish a large book on Rhodes which they propose to call *The Borrowed Island*. Meaning, of course, that they do not regard the island as their own; they just borrow it from various invaders.

The island is charming – perhaps the most pleasant and beautiful of all the Greek islands, and that is saying a great deal. It started to flourish as early as 1306, when the chief admiral of the Byzantine Empire sold it to the Order of

St John of Jerusalem, and it has gone on flourishing ever since. Its walls, its old city, its ancient harbour, its medieval streets and modern quarters, the sea-side, the hills, the ancient Greek ruins – both in the city of Rhodes itself and at Lindos, whose Acropolis is second only to that of Athens – and their excellent hotels, all make it into a little paradise. But all this – and more – may be found in the numerous guide-books. What interested me, particularly, was the life and position of the Turkish minority. Do they really live in such ideal conditions? Do Greeks and Turks really get on with one another so phenomenally well?

The Turks in Cyprus and in Turkey – as I have said before – state that Greeks and Turks are constitutionally incapable of living together; that the favourite pastime of Greeks is to massacre Turks (to which the Greeks retort that it was the Turks who invented genocide). The Greeks, on the other hand, maintain, that the position of their Turkish minorities is ideal, that they enjoy absolute freedom and full minority rights. I should say that the position of the Turks in Rhodes, while not ideal, is quite good – certainly incomparably better than the position of Greeks in Istanbul. The organized massacre of Greeks in that city remains the shame of Turkey. Even today the Greek minority are intimidated; they do not dare to hold public meetings or speak Greek in public. In Rhodes, the Turks may experience some discrimination but no persecution. They speak their language freely; they may worship in their mosques and carry on with their occupations. (Most of them live in the city of Rhodes.) They have their own elementary schools – no higher ones – but Greek, naturally, is a compulsory subject and history and geography are also taught in Greek. There are two Turks on the City Council. One of the best restaurants in Rhodes belongs to a Turk. The place is frequented by tourists and by many Greek Rhodians; by everybody in fact except Turks. Most of the Turks are too poor; but they are in any case forbidden by their religion to eat in the company of unbelievers.

Nevertheless, it is extremely difficult to get information from the Turks. Not only do they not speak freely, they often refuse to speak at all. They are doubly intimidated. They are afraid of the Greek authorities, various repercussions, difficulties with licences, discriminating taxation, etc, but they are also afraid of the local Turkish Consulate, which is said to be very active and whose arm is long. As the local saying has it: the Turks are either organized or terrorized by the Consulate. Many of the Turks in Rhodes have relations in Turkey; many wish to marry Turkish girls from the mainland – thus establishing further ties. So the Consulate can exert pressure. Mysterious Turkish passengers keep arriving in small boats, no one quite knows on what business. But all things considered, the position of the Turks on the Borrowed Island is as good as can be expected; perhaps it may be described as Borrowed Peace.

I gathered two outstanding experiences in Rhodes and, in conclusion, I should like to pass them on.

(1) The first is Turkish in origin and in character. I heard this from the Mufti of Rhodes, a charming and cultured

gentleman of over eighty. He showed me round the mosque and the surrounding cemetery. He stopped in front of three graves and related the following story:

'The Knights of St John evacuated a church when Turkey conquered the island. The Church – according to the custom of those days – was turned into a mosque. No one was aware of the fact that the Knights had left a large amount of gunpowder in the cellar. One day, however, a great storm broke out. Lightning struck the cellar, the gunpowder blew up and killed the keeper, his wife and their little daughter. Their bodies were thrown into the air and found about thirty yards away. They were buried in this cemetery. All this happened in the year 1522.'

The Mufti drew breath.

'In the last war a few bombs fell on Rhodes. One of them hit these three graves and blew the bodies out. They were thrown into the air and were found about thirty yards away. They were reburied here in these new graves. This happened in 1942 – four hundred and twenty years after their first burial.'

There was little need for the Mufti to draw the moral but he did:

'You can't fight your fate. Nothing is in your hands. If your fate is to be blown up, blown up you will be.'

(2) I hired a little self-drive car in Rhodes. Before I drove her away, an official said to me:

'Parking is hell in Rhodes. So is driving in general. But never mind, just park your car anywhere you fancy. And do not hesitate to drive along one-way streets in the wrong direction. You'll collect a large number of tickets, of course. Will you please bring them to my office?'

'That's very kind of you,' I replied, deeply touched, 'but I don't see why you should pay my fines.'

'*Pay?*' The man uttered the word with contempt. 'Who wants to *pay*? We are an official body, you see, and we'll tell the police to tear the tickets up. It's quite all right – and official.'

The moral of this second story is no less clear. Never acquiesce in fate. If your fate is to be fined, there is no need to pay. It all depends on you.

If I may end as a modern Aristotle: This proves once again the ultimate wisdom: do not be too sure of *anything*.

But even scepticism may go too far. Today we have many fanatical sceptics. Do not be too sure even of your doubts: you may be right, after all.

By the same author

HOW TO BE AN ALIEN

HOW TO BE INIMITABLE

HOW TO SCRAPE SKIES

WISDOM FOR OTHERS

MILK AND HONEY

EAST IS EAST

DOWN WITH EVERYBODY!

SHAKESPEARE AND MYSELF

ÜBER ALLES

EIGHT HUMORISTS

LITTLE CABBAGES

ITALY FOR BEGINNERS

TANGO

SWITZERLAND FOR BEGINNERS

*

THE HUNGARIAN REVOLUTION

A STUDY IN INFAMY

*

MORTAL PASSION

a novel